The Homeschool Decision: A Step-By-Step Guide for Parents

By Tiffany Colter, Decision Tree Learning

Copyright ©2024 by Tiffany Colter. All rights reserved.

The Homeschool Decision: A Step-By-Step Guide for Parents. By Tiffany Colter, Decision Tree Learning

You can find additional resources, books, and information on the things in this book by visiting our website

www.DecisionTreeLearning.com

Cover Copyright ©2024 by Tiffany Colter

The scanning, uploading, and distribution of this book without permission is a theft of the author's intellectual property. If you would like permission to use material from the book (other than brief excerpts for review purposes) please contact us using the contact page at www.DecisionTreeLearning.com. Thank you for your support of the author's rights.

Published by Tiffany Colter/Writing Career Coach Press

IBSNs: 978-1-938283-32-1 (paperback); 978-1-938283-36-9 (ebook); 978-1-938283-37-6 (audiobook)

Contents

Chapter 1: Who the Book Is For, How It Is Laid Out, and How It Will Help 11

    Deciding if Homeschooling is Right for You. 11

    Who is This Book For? 11

    The Realities of Homeschooling 12

    The Challenges of Balancing Roles 13

    Making Learning a Way of Life 14

    Defining Your Homeschooling Goals 15

    The Flexibility of Homeschooling 15

    Preparing for the Commitment 16

Chapter 2: Should I Homeschool? Is It Best for My Family? 18

    The Decision to Homeschool 18

    Should I Homeschool? 18

    Will I Commit the Necessary Time? 19

    Can I Dedicate 5-6 Hours a Day? 20

    Will My Child Listen to Me? 20

    Do I Have the Personal Discipline? 21

    Is This the Right Choice for My Child? 21

    Is This the Right Choice for My Family? 22

    Final Thoughts 22

Chapter 3: Why Do You Want to Homeschool? 23

    Understanding Your Motivation 23

    Setting Your Goals as a Homeschooler 24

    Exploring Available Resources 24

Tailoring Homeschooling to Your Child's Needs 25

Moving Forward 25

Chapter 4: How Do You Want to Homeschool? Exploring Philosophies and Methods 27

    Understanding Learning Styles.. 27

    Exploring Homeschooling Philosophies............................. 28

    Unschooling.. 28

    Schooling at Home 29

    Homeschooling Through Local Private Schools 29

    Planning Your Curriculum 30

        Topic Kits... 30

        Project-Based Learning 31

        DVD and Online Curriculum Kits...................................... 31

        Parent-Led Curriculum... 31

        Unschooling (Revisited) 31

    Key Considerations for Your Homeschooling Journey 32

Chapter 5: Where Do You Want to Homeschool?..................... 33

    The Hybrid Model 34

    Other Options 35

    Final Thoughts.. 35

Chapter 6: Reading, Understanding, and Utilizing State Standards and Lesson Examples in Homeschooling................ 36

    The Basics of State Standards... 36

    Accessing and Interpreting Standards 37

    Incorporating State Standards into Lessons.................... 37

    Extending Beyond the Minimum Standards..................... 38

    Addressing Special Educational Needs 38

Balancing Standards and Personal Philosophy 39

Conclusion 39

Chapter 7: What Will I Use to Homeschool? Planning Your Homeschool Curriculum 40

Chapter 8: What Will Your School Day Look Like? Structuring Your Homeschool Day 46

Understanding Your School Day 46

Setting the School Year Calendar 47

Organizing the Learning Environment 48

Utilizing Additional Resources and Community Programs 48

The Importance of Routine 49

Flexibility Within Structure 49

Creating a Focused Learning Environment 50

Balancing Work and Breaks 50

Family Learning and Reading 51

Planning and Organizing Your Homeschool 52

Chapter 9: Constructing the School Day 54

1. Setting Up Your Daily Schedule 54

2. Incorporating Fixed Daily Elements 55

3. Organizing Subject Time 55

4. Implementing and Adjusting Your Plan 56

5. Embracing Flexibility 57

Chapter 10: Creating Lesson Plans and Outcomes 59

Creating Effective Lesson Plans 59

You Don't Need to Be an Expert 60

Balancing New Material 60

Preview, Learn, Review: A Tool for Success 61

Adapting to Different Learning Levels 62

Preparing for Standardized Tests 63

Staying Ahead with Lesson Planning.....................................64

Integrating Field Trips and External Resources 64

Conclusion 65

Chapter 11: Day 1 of Your Homeschool...................................66

Navigating the First Day of Homeschooling..........................66

Getting Started That First Day 67

Chapter 12: Enriching Homeschooling with Field Trips, Videos, and Real-Life Experiences 71

Field Trips: Learning Beyond the Homeschool Classroom 71

Videos: A Visual Learning Tool..72

Incorporating Independent Projects in Your Homeschool.....74

Example of Real-Life Learning: The Grocery Store as a Classroom 74

Enhancing Learning Through Community Resources 75

Conclusion 76

Chapter 13: Learning to Teach 77

The Importance of Writing in Learning 78

Engaging Multiple Senses 78

Improving Your Long-Term Learning with Journals and Notes 79

Solutions for the Challenges of Modern Learning and Why They Are Important 80

Learning Styles: Tailoring Education to Your Child 81

Embracing Mistakes as Part of Learning...............................82

The Value of Quiet Time and Deep Learning 82

Utilizing Resources and Learning from Others 83

Conclusion: Teaching Your Children How to Learn 84

Chapter 14: Assessments and Figuring Out If They Are Learning 85

    Types of Assessments Based on What Is Being Assessed 85

    The Importance of Assessment 86

    Moving Beyond Right and Wrong 87

    Critical Thinking vs. Criticism Thinking 88

    Practical Application in Homeschooling 89

    Encouraging Effort and Resilience 89

Chapter 15: Rubrics and How They Actually Teach Your Kids How to Learn 91

    The Power of Rubrics in Homeschooling 91

    Understanding the Role of Rubrics 91

    Components of an Effective Rubric 92

    Example: The Sidewalk Dilemma 92

    Encouraging Critical Thinking with Rubrics 93

    Involving Students in Rubric Creation 94

    The Lasting Value of Rubrics 94

Chapter 16: *This Isn't What I Thought It Would Be*—Some of the Daily Challenges and Realities of Homeschooling 96

    Everyday Struggles 96

    Technological Challenges 97

    Emotional and Physical Exhaustion for the Homeschooling Parent 97

    Navigating Child Resistance and Diverse Interests 98

    Conclusion 98

Chapter 17: Will My Kids Be Able to Get a Good Job? What About College? 99
   Early Years: Focus on Learning Fundamentals 99
   Transitioning to Middle School: Planning for the Future 100
   High School and Beyond: Tailoring Education for Career Goals 101
   Exploring Opportunities 102
   Embracing the Homeschool Advantage 102

Chapter 18: When Do I Stop Homeschooling? 104
   Preparation for Life 106

Chapter 19: Preparing Your Child for Life Beyond Your Homeschool 108
   The Importance of Life Skills 108
   Incorporating Life Skills into High School Education 110
   Career Exploration and Vocational Training 111
   Encouraging Independence in Your Older Homeschooler ... 112
   Conclusion 113

Chapter 20: Special Considerations 114
   Incorporating Bible Classes into Homeschooling 114
      The Bible as a Historical Document 115
      Key Components of Bible Classes 115
      Remember This is Enjoyable 118
   Integrating Vocational Education into Your Homeschooling 119
      Early Preparation 119
      Understanding Program Requirements 120
      Balancing Vocational Education and Homeschooling 120
      Planning Ahead 121

College Dual Enrollment Options 121
    Understanding Dual Enrollment 121
    Benefits of Dual Enrollment... 122
    How Dual Enrollment Works.. 123
    The Experience of Dual Enrollment 123
Supporting Special Needs Learners 124
    Understanding the Benefits of Homeschooling a Special Needs Learner 124
    Exploring Available Resources..................................... 125
    Seeking Support and Collaboration 126
    Conclusion... 126
Integrating Home Economics and Life Skills 127
    Starting Early 127
    Practical Life Skills... 128
    Advanced Skills and Real-World Applications 129
Career Exploration for Homeschoolers............................... 131
    Introducing Career Exploration 131
    Researching Careers.. 131
    Utilizing Technology and Networking............................ 132
    Job Shadowing and Hands-On Experience 132
    Educational Pathways and Career Requirements 133
    Considering Lifestyle and Job Realities 133
    Preparing for the Future... 133
    Flexibility and Adaptation 134
    Integrating Career Exploration into Homeschooling........ 134
Special Interest Projects in Homeschooling........................ 135

Chapter 21: Mastering Study Skills 138
   Note-Taking and Study Skills 138
   Note-Taking Strategies 138
      Early Elementary.. 138
      Upper Grades 139
   Reviewing Your Notes 139
   Creating Review Materials 140
   Preview, Learn, and Review... 140

Chapter 22: Additional Resources 142
   Field Trip Sheets 142
   Tools to Help Homeschooling Parents 144
      Homeschool Schedule Creation..................................... 144
      The Preview, Learn, Review Tool:.................................. 146
   Rubric Creation Tool and Sample Rubrics......................... 147
      Lower Elementary (1st–3rd Grade) Grading Rubric............ 149
      Upper Elementary (4th-6th Grade) Grading Rubric 150
      Middle School Rubric.. 151
      High School Rubric 152
      College Level Rubric 153

About the Author.. 154
About DecisionTreeLearning.com 156

Chapter 1: Who the Book Is For, How It Is Laid Out, and How It Will Help

Deciding if Homeschooling is Right for You.

Homeschooling is a journey that begins with asking yourself some crucial questions. Whether you're considering homeschooling, currently in the midst of it, or supporting someone who is, this book is for you. It's designed to be a candid guide—sharing the joys, challenges, and practical insights of homeschooling. My hope is that this book will answer many of your questions and provide a safe space for you to explore the realities of homeschooling with honesty and clarity.

Who is This Book For?

This book is for anyone who is curious about homeschooling, has questions, or is actively homeschooling and looking for new strategies. Whether you're considering homeschooling for the first time, or you've been doing it for years, this book offers perspectives that can help you on your journey. It's also for those who support someone who is homeschooling and want to understand how to be more helpful.

If you are currently homeschooling, this book will lay out ideas for lesson plans, grading, assessment, and even special circumstances that you might want to consider in the format of your homeschool.

If you're worried about whether you can properly prepare your kids, then we give you honest questions to consider and solid help if you decide to start.

The Realities of Homeschooling

One of the first and most important questions to ask yourself is: *Is homeschooling right for me*? To answer this, you'll need to consider a few critical factors and be honest with yourself about the answers. Just like parenting, you never feel fully ready and you're always improving. So if that is your biggest worry, rest assured, we all feel that.

The truth is homeschooling demands a significant amount of time and energy. It's not something that can be done casually alongside other responsibilities. When you're homeschooling, you are fully engaged in your children's education, often for six to eight hours a day, depending on the number of children you're teaching. During those hours, you are their teacher, guide, and mentor.

My first year of homeschooling was an eye-opener. Our oldest daughter was five or six years old, with a two-year-old sister and a newborn in tow. I underestimated the time and attention required to nurse a baby, manage a toddler, and teach my oldest daughter. I quickly learned that homeschooling meant being actively engaged with my child, teaching her, showing her how to do things, and guiding her through every step. Even with the curriculum I had bought, she wasn't able to read any of the instructions, so I had to be there to explain how to do each thing.

I had to show her how to use scissors to cut out the art pieces and guide her in forming her letters.

Each stage of homeschooling has its own challenges, but also its own rewards. Being there when she figured out how to sound out words for the first time and sitting together while I read stories to all of the girls is time I would never trade. Two of my three fully homeschooled children went into teaching fields. The love of learning and a desire to help others learn is part of the lasting impact of the years of homeschooling.

The Challenges of Balancing Roles

You might assume that because you're at home, you can easily juggle housework, run errands, or volunteer. But homeschooling is like having a full-time job—one that requires your undivided attention. In those early years, particularly, you are not just overseeing independent work; you are teaching, explaining, and guiding your children every step of the way.

As they grow older, your children will gradually become more independent in their studies, particularly in middle and high school. However, this doesn't mean they'll be teaching themselves. Even then, your role is to guide them, plan lessons, oversee subjects and projects, explain concepts, and be available to answer questions.

For example, teaching long division requires more than just handing over a worksheet. You need to show them the process, practice with them, and be there to answer questions when they struggle. This level of involvement was something I didn't fully anticipate in my early homeschooling days, and it made balancing household responsibilities and teaching incredibly challenging.

There were days when I spent up to ten hours with my head buried in lesson plans, moving from one child to the next. This meant that household chores, grocery shopping, and meal preparation often took a backseat. It was a hard adjustment, and it's one you need to prepare for if you decide to homeschool. You will not be a stay-at-home-parent, you will be a homeschool teacher and a parent.

If you're married, it's important for both you and your spouse to understand that while you'll be at home, you won't be available for typical at-home tasks during school hours. Your priority will be teaching your children. And, unlike what some people like to imply, homeschool parents do not typically pretend that doing household chores and reading a book under a tree is "doing school." While homeschool kids will often help with chores during the day, that is a part of their daily routine, not a part of their school routine—unless they are doing something home economics–specific, which we address later in the book.

Making Learning a Way of Life

One of the beautiful aspects of homeschooling is that learning can become a way of life. In our family, education wasn't confined to textbooks or the hours between 8 a.m. and 3 p.m. We were always learning—whether we were reading books together, watching educational shows, listening to audiobooks, or discussing history and science in everyday conversations, life and learning were always there and the graded segment was what we called school.

Homeschooling allows you to integrate learning into all aspects of life. But to do this effectively, you need to be someone who can embrace this mindset. Are you willing to take the time to research what you need to teach, whether you follow a structured curriculum or create your own lessons?

Defining Your Homeschooling Goals

It's essential to know why you're homeschooling. What is your goal? Your reason for homeschooling should guide your activities and help you achieve the outcomes you desire. Whether you're focused on developing critical thinking skills, supporting a struggling learner, or infusing your education with your faith and values, your approach will need to reflect these priorities.

For example, if one of your goals is to teach financial literacy, you might design a project that involves budgeting and problem-solving. In our homeschool, we did just that. When my daughter expressed an interest in engineering, I gave her a project: build a hydraulic arm with a limited budget. She had to plan, purchase materials, and keep a detailed log of her work. This hands-on experience taught her not only about engineering, but also about budgeting, problem-solving, and the importance of perseverance. Projects are an important part of homeschooling, and I address them multiple times in this book and in other materials I created for homeschoolers. Projects allow you to pull together a variety of subject areas and show how they work together rather than as individual subjects.

In a traditional school setting, the focus is often on getting the right answers and achieving high grades. But in homeschooling, you have the opportunity to prioritize learning over scores. This approach can encourage your children to take risks, learn from failure, and develop a love of learning that extends beyond the classroom.

The Flexibility of Homeschooling

One of the greatest benefits of homeschooling is the flexibility it offers. You don't have to stick to a strict 8 a.m. to 3 p.m.

schedule. If your child learns better in the afternoon or evening, you can adjust your day accordingly. If your work schedule requires you to teach in the evenings or on weekends, homeschooling allows you to make that work.

For our family, the concept of a "school day" was fluid. My husband worked as a paramedic, so our life was structured around his 24-hour shifts. This meant that Saturday might be a school day and Tuesday might be a day off. The only fixed points in our week were church on Sunday and dance lessons on Thursday.

You might need to be creative in how you schedule your homeschooling. Some families adopt a "flipped classroom" model, where the children do some independent work during the day and the parent teaches lessons in the evening. Others might have a more traditional schedule but take breaks throughout the year instead of following the typical school calendar.

> *In a traditional school setting, the focus is often on getting the right answers and achieving high grades. But in homeschooling, you have the opportunity to prioritize learning over scores. This approach can encourage your children to take risks, learn from failure, and develop a love of learning that extends beyond the classroom.*

Preparing for the Commitment

As you consider whether homeschooling is right for you, it's important to ask yourself if you are the right person to homeschool. Homeschooling might be an excellent option for your children, but it requires a significant commitment from you as the parent. You need to be willing and able to make the time and put forth the effort to provide a quality education.

This doesn't mean you can't homeschool if you have a full-time job. It just means you might need to think creatively about how you organize your time and resources. Homeschooling offers the flexibility to make education work for your family, but it also requires discipline and planning.

In the next chapter, we'll explore different homeschooling philosophies and methods, the pros and cons of each, and some of the approaches we tried in our family. I'll share what worked for us, what didn't, and what I learned along the way. Remember, every homeschooling journey is unique, and your approach should reflect your family's needs and goals rather than sticking rigidly to my schedule or someone else's.

As you continue reading, I encourage you to jot down your thoughts and questions. Think about how your life might need to change if you choose to homeschool, what kind of person you need to become to be an effective homeschooling parent, and what your specific goals for homeschooling are.

I look forward to continuing this journey with you and helping you navigate the many decisions that come with homeschooling. Feel free to reach out through the Decision Tree Learning website or Facebook page to share your questions or connect with me. Together, we can explore the possibilities of homeschooling and find the path that's right for you.

www.DecisionTreeLearning.com

Chapter 2: Should I Homeschool? Is It Best for My Family?

The Decision to Homeschool

The decision to homeschool is a significant one, involving various factors that extend beyond just academics. While this book focuses on the academic and practical aspects of homeschooling, it's important to acknowledge that there are numerous other considerations that may influence your choice. Issues such as your local school district, experiences with bullying, special needs, family dynamics, and religious beliefs all play a role in your decision-making process. However, this chapter will concentrate on the foundational questions you should ask yourself if you're contemplating homeschooling.

Should I Homeschool?

The question of whether to homeschool is deeply personal and depends on a variety of factors unique to your situation. One thing to keep in mind is that your decision is not set in stone. Life circumstances change, and what may work for your family now might need to be reassessed in the future.

For example, in our family, we adopted a daughter from another country when she was four and a half years old. She was deaf, and the educational system in her country had classified her as unteachable. When we brought her home, she had no exposure to language or education. Initially, I homeschooled her, but I soon realized that my phonics-based curriculum was not effective for her. We eventually transitioned her into public and later private schools, where she received the support she needed. Meanwhile, I continued to homeschool our other three daughters, each with their own unique educational journeys.

One of my daughters was homeschooled through 10th grade, another through 9th grade, and my youngest up until 7th grade and then again in 11th grade. Each of them had different paths—some continued in private schools, some returned to homeschooling, and one even experienced the transition during the COVID lockdowns. The key takeaway is that homeschooling offers flexibility, and your decision can be revisited as your children's needs and circumstances evolve.

Will I Commit the Necessary Time?

Homeschooling requires a significant time commitment from parents. It's crucial to assess how much time you're willing and able to devote to ensuring your child's education. No parent, regardless of their dedication, can force a child to learn. Your child's motivation will play a role, and homeschooling does not guarantee that they will excel or struggle more than they would in a traditional school setting. Your child's unique personality will still shine through, whether they are homeschooled or attend a public or private school.

As a parent, you must be prepared to invest time in reviewing lessons, selecting or creating curricula, researching resources, visiting libraries, grading papers, and maintaining academic records. Homeschooling goes beyond just sitting down with a workbook. It requires active engagement, especially when your child struggles with certain concepts.

Can I Dedicate 5-6 Hours a Day?

A typical homeschooling day can require five to six hours of your time, though the school year might not follow the traditional August-to-May calendar. In our family, we homeschooled from October to April, allowing flexibility and avoiding the frequent breaks and half days common in public schools. This schedule worked well for us, especially given my husband's unconventional work hours as a paramedic.

Some homeschooling families might take a different approach, such as taking the entire month of December off for family activities and volunteer work. The key is to be consistent on school days. Your children will inevitably ask if they "have to do school today," and while it won't always be met with enthusiasm, your commitment and discipline are essential for success.

Will My Child Listen to Me?

This book aims to be practical, so let's be honest: some children may resist listening to or respecting their parents. If your child is defiant or refuses to do the work, homeschooling may present significant challenges. It's crucial to assess whether you can create an environment conducive to learning. If not, it may be better for your child to be educated in a different setting where they can thrive. However, if your student is falling behind in school because they are not paying attention, having them at home could help. I present the questions; you know your family.

Do I Have the Personal Discipline?

Homeschooling requires a high level of personal discipline, not just from your child, but from you as well. Once you commit to homeschooling for the year, you should aim to follow through. While some parents may pull their children out of school midyear, putting them back in can be much more challenging, leading to gaps in their education that are difficult to overcome.

Your discipline will be tested as you navigate the school year, whether you're working with a set curriculum or a more project-based approach. You need to be prepared to dedicate thirty to thirty-five weeks over the course of the year to your child's education, maintaining consistency even on the days when you don't feel like it.

If you are the type of person who can push through when there is no one looking over your shoulder and you want to homeschool, I absolutely encourage you to do it. It is a very hard thing some days, but it also gives rewards that cannot be articulated sufficiently in this book.

Is This the Right Choice for My Child?

Deciding to homeschool should be based on what is best for your child. Perhaps the academics at their current school aren't meeting their needs, or maybe there are issues that make homeschooling a better option. Whether it's health concerns, personal circumstances, or simply the belief that homeschooling will provide a better education, the decision should center on what will help your child thrive and prepare them for the future.

Is This the Right Choice for My Family?

In addition to considering your child's needs, you must also think about your family dynamic. Will homeschooling be a positive, or at least manageable, experience for your family? If there are significant challenges that might make it difficult to focus on education, consider alternative solutions, such as homeschooling at a library or participating in a co-op for additional support. Don't let a loud apartment or outside distractions deter you from doing it if this is the right option.

Final Thoughts

While these questions may seem daunting, they are designed to help you think critically about whether homeschooling is the right choice for your family. The goal of this book is to guide you through the steps of homeschooling, so you can feel confident in your decision. However, it's essential to approach homeschooling with a realistic mindset. It won't always be smooth sailing, and there will be challenges along the way.

Remember, homeschooling is a significant commitment that requires active participation. You can't effectively homeschool while working full-time or running a business from home without a plan in place. Whether you use a structured curriculum or a more flexible approach, be prepared to invest time and effort into your child's education.

This chapter is just the beginning. In the following chapters, we'll dive deeper into the specifics of homeschooling, helping you navigate the journey with confidence and clarity.

Chapter 3: Why Do You Want to Homeschool?

Understanding Your Motivation

The first step in your homeschooling journey is to clarify why you want to homeschool. Is your decision driven by academic concerns? Do you have specific beliefs or values you want to incorporate into your child's education? Perhaps you want to integrate religious teachings, like the Bible, into your child's learning but prefer not to, or can't afford to, send them to a private school. Maybe you're seeking a deeper, more personalized education, such as a classical curriculum, or there's a family situation—such as frequent travel—that makes homeschooling a more practical option.

These reasons will influence every aspect of your homeschool setup, from the curriculum you choose to the daily schedule you follow. It's important to note that this isn't about justifying your choice to others; it's about using your reasons as a guide to create a learning environment that aligns with your goals and values.

Setting Your Goals as a Homeschooler

Once you understand why you want to homeschool, the next step is to define your goals. There are countless curricula, resources, and teaching methods available, and knowing your goals will help you navigate these options effectively.

For example, if your goal is to provide a robust academic foundation, you'll likely prioritize resources that challenge your child and help them excel in subjects like math and science. On the other hand, if you want to focus on a well-rounded education that includes the arts, humanities, and life skills, you might seek out a more diverse curriculum that includes project-based learning and creative exploration.

Exploring Available Resources

To help you get started, there are numerous online resources that cater to different homeschooling needs. For instance, if your child struggles with a particular subject, such as math, or if you want to ensure they master certain skills, you might consider tools like Elephant Learning or IXL.

Elephant Learning, for example, presents math concepts in a game-like format, making learning feel less intimidating and more engaging. This can be particularly helpful for students who may need some extra encouragement or remediation in math. IXL, on the other hand, offers a broad range of subjects, including math, reading, social studies, and English. It adjusts to the student's learning pace, providing explanations and walkthroughs when they get a problem wrong, which makes it a great tool for self-directed learning.

If your goal is to foster independent learning, you might also find value in traditional paper-and-pencil practice. Keeping a math journal, for example, where students systematically work through problems and write down concepts, can be incredibly beneficial. This approach not only reinforces learning but also encourages students to synthesize information and explain it in their own words—a sign of true mastery.

Tailoring Homeschooling to Your Child's Needs

As you think about your homeschooling approach, consider what will work best for your child. Do they thrive with structure, or do they prefer more freedom to explore their interests? Some students benefit from a structured academic environment with clear goals, while others might excel with a more flexible, project-based learning style.

If your aim is to provide broad exposure to a variety of subjects, you'll want to choose resources that offer a wide range of options. This might include using local libraries, community programs, and other low-cost or free resources to supplement your child's education with research projects and hands-on learning experiences.

Moving Forward

Understanding your reasons for homeschooling and setting clear goals will help you make informed decisions as you move forward. Take some time to jot down your thoughts. Consider keeping a homeschooling journal where you can note why you want to homeschool, how you believe it will benefit your child and family, and any concerns you may have. These reflections will be invaluable as you continue to plan your homeschooling journey. If you have the homeschooling parent lesson planner, *Your Homeschool Blueprint*, there is a place to write these thoughts at the beginning.

Remember, the purpose of this book is to guide you through the steps of homeschooling so you can feel confident in your decision. As you move forward, keep your goals in mind, and use them to shape the learning experience you want to create for your child.

In the next chapter, we'll explore how to address common concerns like socialization and provide practical tips for getting started with homeschooling.

Chapter 4: How Do You Want to Homeschool? Exploring Philosophies and Methods

Homeschooling can seem daunting at first, especially with the numerous approaches available. It's easy to feel overwhelmed, but this chapter aims to guide you through the various homeschooling philosophies step by step. Take your time, reflect on what resonates with you, and remember that once you establish your direction, the process becomes much more manageable.

Homeschooling is not a one-size-fits-all approach. There are several philosophies to consider, each offering unique ways to educate your children. This chapter will introduce you to some of these methods, potentially dispelling any misconceptions you may have. By the end of this chapter, you should have a clearer understanding of the possibilities homeschooling presents, particularly for different types of learners.

Understanding Learning Styles

First, let's acknowledge the different learning styles: visual, auditory, and kinesthetic. Visual learners absorb information best by seeing or reading. Auditory learners prefer listening, while kinesthetic learners thrive through hands-on activities. Recognizing your child's learning style can help you choose the most effective homeschooling approach.

Often you will figure out your child's learning style simply by watching them or as you work with them. What do they do to try to remember things? Are they trying to touch things or do they like audio books? Maybe they always want to write things down. All of these are clues, but also pay attention to them in various subjects. They may use a different learning style to master different subjects. We will have more on this later in the book, but for now, think about it as you watch your child.

In addition to specific learning styles, there are different ways to structure your school day and manner of teaching. I want to briefly touch on this as an introduction. If you want to know more on any of these topics, there are many books that delve as deeply as you would like into each of these.

Exploring Homeschooling Philosophies

There's a broad spectrum of homeschooling philosophies: from unschooling, which is highly unstructured, to schooling at home, which mimics a traditional classroom environment. I won't cover every philosophy or form that homeschooling can take, but rather touch on a few, so you can see the flexibility and start to think about what would work best for you.

Unschooling

Unschooling is often perceived as the most extreme form of homeschooling, where learning is entirely unstructured and child-led. This approach may involve children learning through reading, completing life tasks, and exploring topics of interest without a formal curriculum. While some may view unschooling as chaotic, it can be quite effective for self-motivated learners, allowing them to explore subjects in-depth at their own pace.

In practice, unschooling is usually less extreme than it sounds. It often includes project-based or topic-focused learning. Essential subjects like math, reading, and writing are covered, but the rest of the education may involve documentaries, biographies, fiction, and exploration of various topics in an organic way. This method offers flexibility in scheduling, with learning happening as part of everyday life rather than within a set structure.

Schooling at Home

On the other end of the spectrum is schooling at home, which closely resembles a traditional school day. This approach can be highly structured, with set times for each class, scheduled breaks, and a rigid timetable. The environment might even be separate from the main living area, with a designated homeschool room that mimics a traditional classroom.

This approach can be stressful due to its rigidity, but it provides a clear structure and routine that some children thrive in. The learning material might come from DVDs or online programs, with parents acting as tutors, ensuring their children stay on track.

Homeschooling Through Local Private Schools

Another option is homeschooling under the supervision of a local private school. In this arrangement, a private school provides oversight by reviewing your child's work and ensuring they meet certain academic standards. This option offers a middle ground, where the child is homeschooled but can still participate in certain extracurricular activities like choir, sports, or school plays offered by the private school. Additionally, students may receive a diploma from the private school, which can simplify the college admissions process.

Planning Your Curriculum

One of the most common concerns about homeschooling is knowing what to teach. This will be covered in more detail in the lesson-planning chapter, but to ease your worries, here are some basics.

Each state has educational standards that outline what students should learn at each grade level. If you wish to create your own curriculum, these standards can serve as a guideline. However, most homeschooling parents do not write their entire curriculum from scratch. Instead, they often use a core curriculum supplemented by additional projects or resources tailored to their child's interests and needs.

Here are some common types of curricula you might encounter:

Topic Kits

These are prepackaged sets that cover all subjects around a specific theme. For example, a chocolate-themed kit might explore the science of chocolate production, the history of chocolate in trade and culture, and even math lessons involving measurements related to chocolate. Most are not as simplistic as this and can be much more involved and cover broader topics, but they can also be this specific, which is great if a child has a particular area of interest.

Project-Based Learning

This approach involves giving your child a specific project to work on, sometimes over an extended period. Projects might focus on research, building, or exploring a particular interest. This method teaches valuable skills such as budgeting, planning, and problem-solving. It also emphasizes that failure is a part of learning, encouraging children to try different approaches until they find a solution that works.

DVD and Online Curriculum Kits

Many homeschooling families use DVD or online courses. These programs often come with textbooks, lesson plans, and grading guides. Parents act as facilitators, providing help when needed but allowing their children to work independently.

Parent-Led Curriculum

This method involves the parent taking full control of the curriculum, planning and teaching all lessons. While some parents choose to write every lesson themselves, most prefer to use a mix of prewritten curricula and their own additions. This approach allows for maximum flexibility and customization.

Unschooling (Revisited)

As mentioned earlier, unschooling is highly flexible and often involves child-led learning. Parents provide resources and opportunities, but the child directs their own education. This approach can be liberating but requires a lot of trust in the child's ability to learn and grow independently.

Key Considerations for Your Homeschooling Journey

As you think about what you want your homeschool to look like, consider the following questions:

- What key skills do you want your child to master beyond the basics?

- How will you structure your days to balance learning with flexibility?

- What materials and resources will you use to support your child's education?

- What topics are your children passionate about, and how can you incorporate those interests into their learning?

Remember, homeschooling offers the unique opportunity for your children to become active participants in their education rather than passive recipients. Embrace the flexibility, and let your homeschool evolve in a way that best supports your family's needs and your children's individual learning styles.

Chapter 5: Where Do You Want to Homeschool?

When we hear the term "homeschool," it's easy to assume that education is confined to the walls of your home. However, as we've touched on in earlier discussions, homeschooling can extend far beyond your living room or kitchen table.

Homeschooling can incorporate co-ops, online learning, and group activities where parents share teaching responsibilities.

In some families, parents with different skills and expertise come together to create a well-rounded educational experience. For example, one family might have a father who is an engineer, while another has a parent skilled in a trade like construction or law. These families may decide to "trade off" teaching duties, creating a co-op where parents alternate teaching groups of children in their areas of expertise. This arrangement not only diversifies the children's learning experience but also fosters a sense of community among the families involved.

Co-ops can take various forms. The most common model involves groups that meet once a week for a set period. During these sessions, parents take turns teaching different subjects. This might mean one parent leads a history unit for all the children while another focuses on science. These co-ops offer a great opportunity for parents to introduce their children to subjects they might not feel comfortable teaching themselves.

For instance, a parent with a degree in chemistry might put together a series of science lessons, while another with a passion for cooking could lead a culinary class.

The area I lived in, a rural part of Michigan, had a large homeschooling population, which led to the formation of various groups that provided extracurricular activities typically associated with traditional schools. These groups organized sports teams that played against local private schools, hosted proms, and offered classes in subjects like physical education and health. They met in diverse venues, from churches to community centers, and gave children the chance to learn about things their parents might not have been well-versed in.

The Hybrid Model

Another option for homeschooling families is the hybrid model with a private school. This model involves the private school having some level of oversight over the homeschool, which can make some homeschooling families nervous. In our experience, this meant submitting lesson plans monthly to a designated homeschool coordinator at the private school. We would meet with them once a month, where I would outline our teaching plans and present samples of the previous month's work. This wasn't a judgmental process; rather, it felt like a supportive exchange with a licensed teacher who could offer guidance and feedback. The private school also provided a diploma upon completion, which is something public schools typically do not offer in similar oversight arrangements. There was a small fee associated with this arrangement, but it gave our daughter the right to participate in school activities and certain classes like art or music at the school building.

Other Options

Online homeschooling is another approach, though I personally don't consider online public school programs as true homeschooling. While these programs allow children to learn from home, parents have little control over the curriculum, which is a stark contrast to the freedom and flexibility that homeschooling traditionally offers.

Beyond these models, there are many other ways to enrich your homeschooling experience. Community groups, like 4-H, can be incorporated into your homeschool curriculum, offering specialized learning experiences. There are also large, organized homeschooling groups that offer a wide range of social and extracurricular activities, including sports teams, dances, and other events. These groups provide all the social components typically associated with public or private schools, but within a homeschooling framework.

Final Thoughts

If you're considering homeschooling, think about where you want your child's education to take place—not just at home, but in terms of off-site activities and community involvement. Research local homeschooling groups and national organizations that can connect you with resources and communities in your area. By doing so, you can create a homeschooling experience that not only meets your educational goals but also includes the social and extracurricular opportunities that many of us cherished in our own school years.

Chapter 6: Reading, Understanding, and Utilizing State Standards and Lesson Examples in Homeschooling

In this chapter, we will explore how to effectively use state standards to guide your homeschooling efforts without becoming overwhelmed. You don't have to feel intimidated or overwhelmed when you start to try to use these. In fact, I have found that the state standards have made the job of teaching easier by giving me a clear guide and example. I am using Ohio as an example, but be sure to check the standards in your state. I will show you how these standards can help shape your lesson plans and ensure a quality education for your children.

As I have said before, most standard curriculum will already meet these standards, but if you're creating your own or you are concerned about missing a requirement, I've included this lesson to help you.

The Basics of State Standards

State education boards, such as Ohio's, outline specific requirements for each grade level. These standards are generally consistent across states and provide a framework for what students should learn. However, you don't need to memorize every detail. Instead, focus on the overarching goals and key components.

Accessing and Interpreting Standards

Start by reviewing your state's educational standards and model curricula. These documents outline the educational goals and the subjects to be covered. For instance, Ohio provides a model curriculum that includes subjects like computer science, English language arts, financial literacy, and world languages.

You can also look under the special education tab to find what is called "Extended Standards," which explain the standards for students with various learning disabilities and cognitive or communication challenges. If your student is struggling in a particular area, I have found these to be an excellent resource to help you break down the learning to its component pieces and then build back up to more and more difficulty.

If your state's resources are limited or unclear, feel free to use Ohio's website to help you. They provide standards as well as examples to guide your lesson planning.

https://education.ohio.gov/Topics/Learning-in-Ohio

https://education.ohio.gov/Topics/Learning-in-Ohio/Financial-Literacy/Elementary-Grades

Incorporating State Standards into Lessons

State standards often provide a basic framework for subjects, including essential topics such as financial literacy. For example, Ohio's financial literacy curriculum for elementary grades includes topics like financial responsibility, decision-making, and the use of credit. The model curriculum outlines general expectations, such as understanding the role of money in transactions and responsible borrowing.

You can use these guidelines to create engaging lessons. For instance, the guidelines require a lesson on credit and debt for young students, which simply means explaining different payment methods—like cash and credit cards—and discussing responsible borrowing. Incorporate real-life examples, such as managing an allowance or understanding sales tax, to make these concepts relatable.

Extending Beyond the Minimum Standards

While state standards provide a useful baseline, they are not exhaustive. Feel free to expand on these standards by incorporating your own educational goals and philosophies. For instance, if you have strong views on financial management or charitable giving, integrate these into your lessons. This personal touch not only enriches the learning experience but also aligns with your values.

Addressing Special Educational Needs

As I alluded to earlier, one benefit of state standards is helping your child if they have particular academic difficulties. State standards or resources specifically designed for diverse learners can give you ideas to help break a topic down. These resources help tailor educational content to various learning abilities, from simpler to more complex tasks.

For example, if a student struggles with basic math concepts, you can use extended standards to break down the material into manageable parts. Start with foundational concepts and gradually increase the complexity as the student progresses.

This approach helps accommodate different learning speeds and ensures that each student can achieve success at their own pace.

Balancing Standards and Personal Philosophy

Remember, state standards are tools to aid your teaching, not to restrict it. You have the flexibility to adapt and enhance your lessons according to your child's needs and your educational philosophy. Share your reasoning and perspectives with your child, allowing them to understand different viewpoints and develop critical thinking skills.

Conclusion

Incorporating state standards into your homeschooling routine does not need to be daunting. These standards are designed to support your educational goals and provide a structured approach to teaching. By focusing on the key components and supplementing with your own insights, you can deliver a comprehensive and engaging education to your children. Embrace the flexibility and creativity that homeschooling offers and use state standards as a guide rather than a constraint.

Chapter 7: What Will I Use to Homeschool? Planning Your Homeschool Curriculum

When beginning your homeschooling journey, one of the first questions to address is: *What will I use to homeschool?* In this chapter, we'll dive deeper into the materials and methods you'll employ in your homeschooling approach. By the end, you'll have a clearer idea of the subjects to cover, some of which you may have already considered, while others might be new to you. This list is by no means exhaustive—there are countless electives and other subjects available online.

First, consider *how* you want to teach your child. For example, you might prefer a structured curriculum for subjects like math, where a systematic, step-by-step approach can be beneficial. There are numerous resources, including websites like DecisionTreeLearning.com, where you can find tools to supplement your teaching.

On the other hand, there might be subjects, such as literature, where you want to take a more hands-on approach. As a professional writer with a passion for reading, literature was a subject I wanted to guide myself. I selected specific books that I wanted my children to read and discuss, focusing on certain ideas and themes. Of course, they were welcome to explore other books on their own time, but I wanted to direct the core of their literature education.

You might feel similarly about a subject you're passionate about, especially if it's related to your area of expertise. For instance, if your background is in natural sciences, you might prefer to teach those subjects without relying heavily on a set curriculum, choosing instead to design your own lessons.

I found that in the early years, I was more comfortable using a standard curriculum to make sure my kids had a very strong foundation, and I didn't forget something. Those early years were also some tough ones, so, on occasion, we couldn't afford to buy the specific curriculum I wanted to use, and I had to adapt.

As they got older—in middle school and high school—I felt more comfortable, and added supplemental courses outside of the core academics, with curriculum I created and designed. I also felt much more comfortable in my ability to design assessments that helped me to test for the results I felt were critical to mastering the subject rather than standard systems of grading homework and/or assignments. To do this, I drew on things I'd learned from other public-school teachers and homeschoolers. This can seem intimidating to some, so I have a section on this later in this book.

As you plan, keep in mind the structure of your lessons. Aim for lessons that last no more than thirty minutes. It's a common misconception that homeschooling requires filling seven or eight hours of the day with instruction.

In reality, your day should focus on a few key subjects, each covered in a fifteen-to-thirty-minute lesson. The rest of the time should be spent on activities that reinforce the lesson, such as reviewing material, completing worksheets, or engaging in related assignments.

In traditional school settings, actual teaching time often amounts to only twenty to thirty minutes per class, even in high school. Since your child doesn't need to wait for others' questions to be answered, you can cover material more efficiently. Your lessons should be concise, focusing on the essential points, with five to seven subjects covered each day—unless you are doing block scheduling where you meet for longer periods, but less frequently.

Remember to include subjects like physical education and health. For younger children, this might involve hands-on learning, such as meal planning and preparation. Activities like helping you make dinner can be a valuable part of their education, falling under home economics or health classes.

Another important consideration is how to manage your homeschooling schedule, especially if you have multiple children. When I first started homeschooling my children, I quickly realized that I couldn't teach all of them simultaneously. Each child had different books, topics, and academic levels, so I had to create a schedule that allowed for individual instruction as well as self-guided work. Some days, I worked one-on-one with a child, while other days, they focused on independent study, reviewing their work and coming to me with questions.

> **Don't overplan**
>
> As you plan, keep in mind the structure of your lessons. Aim for lessons that last no more than thirty minutes. It's a common misconception that homeschooling requires filling seven or eight hours of the day with instruction.

When organizing your homeschool, consider how much time each child will need for independent study versus direct instruction. Encourage them to work through problems on their own before coming to you for help. This approach fosters independence and critical thinking. When they do seek your assistance, guide them to understand where they might have made a mistake or what they did correctly up to a certain point. By doing this, instead of simply telling them the answer, they can try to duplicate the process to go back to the foundational component and build back up. This results in them eventually figuring out how to figure something out. It is like sounding out a word, but on a bigger scale.

So, what will you use to homeschool each subject? Below, I've provided a list of subjects and space for you to jot down notes. I recommend keeping a homeschool binder where you can organize your ideas and plans. This binder will be a valuable tool for tracking your curriculum choices, resources, and schedules.

If you have specific resources in mind—such as a particular curriculum or online platform—write those down as well, along with the subject they'll be used for. For example, if you want to use a program like Great Courses for history, specify which courses you're interested in, such as "History of Greece." Getting specific will help you with budgeting, time management, and avoiding unnecessary purchases.

In the first few years of homeschooling, it's easy to overbuy, especially if you're creating your own curriculum. Focus on what you truly need for each grade level and remember to schedule time for enrichment activities like art and music. These can be integrated into your day in creative ways, such as listening to audiobooks while your children are working on art projects, followed by group discussions.

As you plan, consider each child's individual needs and make sure your schedule allows time for both group and independent activities. Organizing your homeschool thoughtfully will set the foundation for a successful and enjoyable learning experience for your family.

When I was first homeschooling, I worried I would miss a subject or important area. If you are like me and would like to use a more structured curriculum, there are many available. I used the Abeka DVD curriculum later in my homeschooling journey, but in the early years I used parent-led Abeka curriculum and other subject-based programs drawn from a variety of sources.

One thing I really enjoyed was our enrichment year, which I was only able to do with my oldest. She had five years of high school, with an enrichment year between 10th and 11th grade where we emphasized areas of interest, career exploration, and life skills. This allowed us to meet state requirements for high school graduation while also allowing her considerable time to develop skills and learning for life beyond school.

Subjects:

- Reading [the skill and literature/critical thinking]
- Writing [penmanship and essays]
- Math [both theory/skills and life/consumer math]
- Science
- Social studies/current events
- Critical thinking [not criticism thinking, more on that later]
- Literature analysis
- Penmanship

- Typing
- Cursive [more on that later]
- Music/arts
- Physical education
- Home education
- Foreign language
- Computer literacy
- Bible

Chapter 8: What Will Your School Day Look Like? Structuring Your Homeschool Day

"Researchers found that children from structured homeschool settings outperformed their conventional school peers (by 0.06 to 0.15 effect sizes)." Davidson citing Martin-Chang et al., 2011 [Full citation at the end of this chapter]

If a structured homeschool setting helps students, then let's look at what that means. What is a structured setting and how can you turn your homeschool in to one?

Understanding Your School Day

When planning your homeschool day, it's essential to determine the basic structure—including start and finish times, the length of each subject, and when to schedule breaks throughout the day and throughout the school year. Unlike traditional schools, homeschooling allows you to customize your schedule according to your family's needs. This flexibility is one of the key benefits of homeschooling, so take advantage of it. For example, you might decide that art deserves more time than penmanship. Or perhaps your child is more focused in the morning, so you start early and finish by lunchtime. The choice is yours. As you will hear me say multiple times, the key is consistency and clear expectations. Your kids need to know when it is school time and when it is free time. Being ambiguous with schedules is a fast way to get students to resist doing their schoolwork.

Just as with a public or private school, there will be occasions where you need to have a half day, miss part of the day for an appointment, or start late. I really feel it is important to clearly articulate to the kids that this is an exception and let your habits line up with your words—make them an exception. You may even want to go so far as to have a monthly school calendar which shows daily start/end times, appointments, and special field trips/outings separately from the family calendar. While not every student needs this much division, at least one of my kids really benefitted from having that kind of clarity, and it also taught all of the kids about time management.

Setting the School Year Calendar

Planning doesn't stop at the daily schedule; you also need to think about your school year calendar. Decide when your school year will start and end and consider the timing of vacations and breaks. In public schools, students typically have two to three weeks off during the Christmas and New Year holidays, along with a spring break. However, in other countries and even within different school districts in the U.S., school calendars vary widely. Some schools operate year-round with shorter breaks scattered throughout the year or do a co-op schedule where a student alternates between school and work.

As a homeschooler, you have the freedom to create a calendar that works best for your family. You might choose to take a longer break during a season when your family travels or work commitments are lighter. The key is to find a balance that maintains consistency in your child's education while accommodating your family's lifestyle.

Organizing the Learning Environment

The physical space where your homeschooling takes place is just as important as your schedule. Consider where you will keep supplies, books, and other materials. In the early days of homeschooling, you might start with a simple setup, such as a bookshelf in the dining room where each child has their own shelf. As your homeschool evolves, you might designate a specific room or area for schooling.

For instance, some families create a dedicated homeschool room with individual desks and storage areas for each child. Others may homeschool at the kitchen table, with materials stored nearby. It's also worth thinking about how accessible your teacher resources are. You might keep answer keys in a separate location to maintain the integrity of testing and grading.

Whatever your setup, it should be organized in a way that supports your teaching and your child's learning. I have read many articles that say it is better not to store the materials, particularly your teaching materials, in your bedroom because it can interfere with sleep. I never had room in my bedroom to store my materials, although I did keep the grading keys under my bed one year, but I share it in case it is helpful for you to consider that.

Utilizing Additional Resources and Community Programs

Homeschooling isn't confined to your home. Zoos, parks, community programs, and co-ops can all play a significant role in your child's education. Take time to think about how you will integrate these external resources into your homeschool. You might schedule regular trips to the zoo or participate in a local co-op where your child can interact with other homeschoolers. These activities not only enrich your child's learning but also provide socialization opportunities.

The Importance of Routine

While flexibility is one of homeschooling's strengths, consistency is equally important. Establish a routine that your children can rely on. Even if the start time varies from day to day, try to keep a consistent schedule for each specific day of the week. For example, your Monday routine could include math in the morning, followed by a break, and then language arts. Tuesday might start with science and then move on to history.

Children thrive when they know what to expect, and a consistent routine helps create a stable learning environment. However, remember that routines should serve your family's needs, not the other way around. Adjust as necessary but maintain a general structure that provides stability.

Flexibility Within Structure

One of the most significant advantages of homeschooling is the ability to adapt to your child's learning pace. If your child masters a subject quickly, allow them to move on or take a break. On the other hand, if they struggle with a concept, give them the time they need to understand it fully without the pressure of a strict schedule.

Avoid overscheduling your days with back-to-back activities, leaving no room for flexibility. If your school day is supposed to end at 2:00 p.m., but you have an extracurricular activity scheduled for 3:00 p.m., make sure there's enough time to transition without rushing. Build in buffer time so that learning doesn't feel hurried or stressful.

Creating a Focused Learning Environment

Your children should do their schoolwork in a space where you can supervise and support them, rather than in their bedrooms. This not only helps keep them focused but also allows you to monitor their progress and be available for questions. During school hours, try to model good work habits yourself. Sit nearby, perhaps planning lessons or working on something that can be easily interrupted. This shows your children that you take their education seriously and are there to support them.

However, be mindful of your own tasks during school time. If you're working on something that requires intense concentration, interruptions might lead to frustration, which isn't conducive to a positive homeschooling environment. Choose activities that allow you to be available and approachable for your children.

Balancing Work and Breaks

While it's important for children to have breaks throughout the day, be intentional about their use of time. If a child completes a task early, they might use that time for reading, working on a long-term project, or simply taking a short break. Teach them the value of managing their time effectively, so they don't feel like they're just "punching a clock." What I mean is there is no reason to require a student to continue to sit at a table simply because it is the time of day when they "have to do school." That is something done in a school building because of scheduling, but not at home. Instead, have ongoing projects they can work on during that extra free time. Also, be diligent in watching how quickly they complete their work. Are they rushing and doing poor quality work? If so, that is a teachable moment. Is the work too easy for them? Then allow them to have other more challenging work.

Homework in a homeschool setting can be a bit of a misnomer since all their work is technically done at home. However, assigning tasks that help reinforce what was learned during the day, such as reading, creating review sheets, or working on a project, can be beneficial. Projects that span several weeks or even a semester can help teach time management and the ability to break down large tasks into manageable parts.

I am a huge advocate of using projects in homeschools because it gives children skills they will use in college or on the job. Effectively learning to manage their time and break larger assignments into component parts is extremely valuable, so you'll hear me mention it often. Many college students don't know how to make a small set of tasks from a larger project, and it creates unnecessary stress and poor performance. This can be very discouraging and lead to an otherwise intelligent student quitting school. Teaching students to take the lead in creating and completing their projects also allows for creativity and responsibility.

Family Learning and Reading

Consider integrating family reading into your homeschool routine. Reading the same book as a family, or choosing books on similar topics for each child, can create shared learning experiences. For example, younger children might focus on the story's characters, while older ones delve into historical contexts or thematic elements. This not only strengthens family bonds but also enriches the educational experience.

And don't worry if you are reading the same books multiple times over successive years. How many times have they watched the same movie more than once? They will get something new out of the second reading—and third. One question can actually be: *What did you notice this time that you didn't notice in the past?*

Incorporating audiobooks can also be an excellent way to engage children in learning while you're occupied with other tasks, like cooking or cleaning. It allows the whole family to enjoy a story together and discuss it afterward, making learning a collaborative and enjoyable experience.

I always had audio books running in the kitchen, the car, during afternoon quiet time in their rooms. Books were a huge part of the lives of all my children and so were times at the library.

Planning and Organizing Your Homeschool

As you prepare for homeschooling, take time to organize your plans and materials. Whether you use a notebook, a digital planner, or a specialized homeschool planning book, keeping everything organized is crucial. Jot down ideas, plan lessons, and think through the activities that excite you and your children.

Remember, homeschooling is a journey, and it's okay to make adjustments as you go. The key is to create an environment and routine that supports both your child's learning and your family's unique lifestyle.

Note:

Brian D. Ray (2017) A systematic review of the empirical research on selected aspects of homeschooling as a school choice, Journal of School Choice, 11:4, 604-621,

DOI: 10.1080/15582159.2017.1395638

To link to this article:
https://doi.org/10.1080/15582159.2017.1395638

Chapter 9: Constructing the School Day

Creating a structured yet flexible homeschool day is key to ensuring that both you and your students remain organized and focused. This chapter will guide you through the process of constructing an effective school day, incorporating tools and strategies to help you manage your time and responsibilities efficiently.

1. Setting Up Your Daily Schedule

Begin by developing a subject check sheet for each student for each day. A sample of this sheet can be found in the tools section at the back of this book. The check sheet should include all subjects, including physical education activities like dance, co-op classes, and any other out-of-home activities. It's crucial to account for these external commitments as they will impact your daily schedule.

Make sure to factor in commute times for activities outside the home. Since daily schedules may vary, it is important to include a designated section for each student on their individual check sheet. For students who will be traveling with you, allocate time accordingly and plan for activities they can do during the commute that are suited to the environment.

2. Incorporating Fixed Daily Elements

Identify any immovable elements in your daily routine. For instance, if you have a newborn who naps at a specific time each day, plan to schedule activities that require less direct supervision during that nap time. For example, use this period for art projects or handwriting practice rather than subjects requiring your immediate involvement, such as math or reading.

If you don't have such constraints, consider how you might structure time for activities that involve all students together. This could include group activities such as art, music, or physical education, or participation in co-op classes where the entire family is engaged simultaneously.

3. Organizing Subject Time

Next, plan out each child's subjects, ensuring that you allocate specific times for each lesson. One effective method is to use color-coded construction paper or index cards to represent different types of lessons:

- *RED*: Classes requiring full engagement from you.
- *PINK*: Classes where you provide instructions while students work independently.
- *YELLOW*: Independent work or activities where students work on their own with minimal oversight.
- *GREEN*: Activities requiring minimal or no direct involvement from you.

Label each card or paper with the child's name and the subject. This color-coding system helps you visualize and organize the daily schedule effectively. If a subject, like science, requires different types of engagement on different days, use multiple colors to represent these variations.

I prefer to make a large sheet of paper for each day and then line them up on the table with names across the top and times down the side. The index cards correspond to each class meeting time for that subject. If it is easier to see this in color, go to DecisionTreeLearning.com to see it in the blog archives.

MONDAY	Linda 4th	Jarred 2nd	Tony Kindergarten
9am	Linda Math lesson	Jarred Art Lesson	Tony Eating Breakfast; Starts at 10am
10am	Linda Math review and Penmanship	Jarred Copy down spelling words	Tony Phonics and Reading
11am			
Noon			

Cut out index cards or construction paper for each subject and arrange them on a large sheet of paper or board.

4. Implementing and Adjusting Your Plan

Once you've created your schedule, use it to guide your daily routine. Snap a picture of your completed schedule for easy reference. Be prepared to make adjustments as needed. Your initial plan will likely require modifications as you see what works and what doesn't. It is normal for schedules to evolve based on the time required for different subjects or changes in the students' needs. Flexibility is key—some subjects may take more or less time than anticipated, and you may need to reorder or adjust activities based on your family's dynamic and daily experiences.

5. Embracing Flexibility

Understand that your schedule should serve as a guideline rather than a rigid structure. Adjustments are a natural part of the homeschooling process. If you find that some subjects or activities need more time or if the daily flow is disrupted, make the necessary changes to maintain balance and avoid burnout. But it is rarely necessary to completely remake the schedule. The only time I ever had to completely flip things around was when I realized that one of my daughters was burning out at the end of the day during reading time. I moved her reading time earlier in the day and then made room in my schedule to work more directly with her during that time and it worked out much better. Instead, she ended the day with art, which was a reward after a long day of work.

It is also acceptable to have gaps in the schedule for breaks, late starts, or early releases. Many public schools have similar adjustments, and it is perfectly fine to incorporate these into your homeschool routine. For my girls, it was on Thursdays when we had to leave the house early to pick up our daughter attending public school so that we could make it in time for dance lessons. I put the electives at the end of the day, so if they were running behind, we could easily take those lessons with us in the car. The goal is to create a schedule that supports effective learning while accommodating your family's unique needs.

In summary, constructing a successful homeschool day involves careful planning, color-coded organization, and flexibility. By using these strategies, you can create a balanced and effective learning environment that adapts to the needs of both you and your students.

Chapter 10: Creating Lesson Plans and Outcomes

Creating Effective Lesson Plans

Creating lesson plans and setting educational outcomes might seem intimidating at first, but it doesn't have to be. If you're using a textbook for a subject, much of the planning is already done for you. Your main task will be to supplement the textbook with additional materials that enhance learning based on your child's unique needs and determining what days each lesson will be done.

If you are creating your own curriculum and lesson plans from scratch, there is more involved; but the key is knowing what you want your student to learn, how you are going to teach that skill, how you will have them practice the skill, and how you want to evaluate their understanding of the skill. That is really what a learning outcome is.

Now, having said that, it isn't always easy. For example, how do you teach gravity? Do you want to teach about people in the history of science, or focus on scientific principles? Do you want them to learn using primary sources or secondary sources like textbooks? It can be as simple or as complex as you decide to make it—but try not to be intimidated by it. Stay focused on the basics.

You Don't Need to Be an Expert

It's important to remember that you don't have to be an expert in every subject, nor do you need to write textbooks to successfully homeschool your children. Even teachers in traditional schools rely on textbooks and then add in additional materials to reinforce the learning. Your job is to find textbooks that do an excellent job of covering the material and then add supplemental resources to address your child's specific learning needs or parts you'd like to emphasize. The one area where it could be difficult to teach is one that isn't widely covered by traditional textbooks or is on very specific/niche topics. In those cases, just go back to the list I gave you:

- WHAT do you want your student to learn?
- HOW are you going to teach that skill?
- HOW will you have them practice the skill?
- HOW will you evaluate their understanding?

Balancing New Material

As you plan your school day, ensure you have time to introduce new material to each child. A key strategy is to avoid introducing entirely new topics in every subject on the same day. For example, let's consider a 4th grade student named Tiffany. She might have subjects like reading, English, math, science, and social studies, as well as classes like library, art, music, and PE. You wouldn't want to introduce brand new concepts in reading, English, math, and science all on the same day. Instead, you could plan for a day where reading involves free reading time,

English introduces a new part of speech, and science reviews the scientific method.

The goal is to ensure that Tiffany is only dealing with completely unfamiliar information in one or two subjects at a time, which reduces stress and helps her focus better. This approach is especially beneficial for elementary students, where a single teacher typically staggers the introduction of new topics. For high school students, you can push them a bit more, but even then, it's best not to overwhelm them by introducing too many new topics at once, unless the skill is stress and time management [both completely reasonable high school skills], in which case you can periodically have a more intense few days to teach them how to work through the stress.

Preview, Learn, Review: A Tool for Success

To help you visualize and plan your lessons, I developed a tool called Preview, Learn, Review. You can find it in the back of this book. I've also created a separate book with these resources in an easy-to-use format, available both in print and as an e-

Learning Outcome

If you are creating your own curriculum and lesson plans from scratch, there is more involved; but the key is knowing what you want your student to learn, how you are going to teach that skill, how you will have them practice the skill, and how you want to evaluate their understanding of the skill. That is really what a learning outcome is.

book. If you prefer, you can copy the information from this book into your own journal or notebook.

The Preview, Learn, Review tool is designed to help you decide when to introduce new topics, ensuring that your student is neither overwhelmed nor under-challenged. The process is simple:

1. *Preview* the material to give your student exposure to key concepts and vocabulary before they dive into learning.

2. *Learn* the material through structured lessons.

3. *Review* the material afterward to reinforce understanding and retention.

This method can be applied on a broad scale across the school year, as well as on a more general level, such as daily or weekly lessons. Public schools often use a similar approach, where the first several weeks of the school year are spent reviewing and ensuring mastery of the previous year's material before moving on to new content, and then reviewing material in the spring just before standardized tests begin.

Adapting to Different Learning Levels

While public schools follow a general structure, as a homeschooling parent, you have the flexibility to tailor this process to your child's individual needs. This is particularly important if you have a child with special learning needs. Many state education boards offer detailed guidelines that break down learning objectives for different levels, from advanced students to those with significant challenges. These guidelines can be a valuable resource, providing practical examples to help you understand what your student needs to learn and how to achieve those goals. I am familiar with the extended standards for the state of Ohio and really love how clear they are to read. Furthermore, they have great sample curricula and other resources on their website.

I have not extensively researched extended standards or learning outcomes in other states, but check your state's website. You can also look at Ohio's standards because many states are very similar. If you need lesson plan ideas, I found these very helpful, and you might find them helpful for developing your homeschooling lessons too.

Preparing for Standardized Tests

If your child is on a college track, it's important to start introducing standardized tests around middle school. This isn't just about preparing for college entrance exams, but also about developing the test-taking skills that homeschoolers might not naturally acquire. Test taking is a skill in itself, and some students who excel in learning may struggle with standardized testing if they haven't practiced. In public school, students grow very accustomed to test taking, while homeschoolers do not. When I attended public school, we started practicing for the PSATs in the 9th grade, even though we didn't yet have the knowledge to answer many of the questions; it was just so we got more familiar and comfortable with the format of the test. Start with practice tests to build these skills without the pressure of reviewing an entire year's worth of material.

If your child doesn't plan to go to college, then find out the kinds of skills and licensing tests they need to be comfortable with, so they have a better shot of success. Fire fighters, police, postal workers, skilled trades workers, cosmetologists, and many other careers have testing or licensing requirements, whether or not they require a college degree. Finding preparation books for those licensing exams and giving your child an opportunity to get familiar with the format can be a very useful part of your high school homeschool curriculum.

Staying Ahead with Lesson Planning

When working with a curriculum, whether it's one you've created or one from a textbook, it's crucial to stay ahead of your students. I recommend being at least two to four weeks ahead in your reading and lesson planning. This allows you to anticipate upcoming topics and ensures you're prepared to teach them effectively. [Remember: Preview, Learn, Review.]

If you're less confident in a particular subject area, this advanced preparation gives you time to study up or find additional resources to support both you and your student in learning. You will also find it easier to plan for field trips, outings, or other activities by being ahead and trying to have a field trip that covers material that all of your children would benefit from. Working ahead and knowing what is being covered will help you do that.

Integrating Field Trips and External Resources

Consider how field trips and external resources can be integrated into your lesson plans. For example, if you're covering a specific historical period, a visit to a local museum could enhance your child's understanding. If you're studying biology, a trip to the zoo could bring the subject to life. When planning field trips, think about how they can complement what all your children are learning, especially if they're at different grade levels. This way, you can make the most of the experience without disrupting your school schedule.

But what if only one child is covering the topic? The majority of homeschool families have three or more children homeschooling simultaneously, so you are in good company. Look at this example:

4 kids in kindergarten, 3rd, 5th, and 7th grade. You are planning a wintertime trip to the art museum.

The 7th and 5th grader will be asked to look at pictures from a particular style, medium, or artist. Let's say, African pottery. They will complete their field trip sheet with that assignment. The 7th grader has the added assignment of researching the piece and writing a three-paragraph essay about what they learned in their research.

The 3rd grader will identify three different mediums [example: clay pottery, paint, and wood]

The kindergartener will pick a favorite piece of art and dictate to you what they like about it and why.

Conclusion

By following the Preview, Learn, Review method and staying organized with your lesson plans, you can create a successful and stress-free homeschooling environment. Remember to use the tools and resources available to you, whether they're in this book, on my website, or from other educational resources. If you have any questions or need further guidance, I'm here to help. Visit my website at DecisionTreeLearning.com and let me know how you're doing. Now we'll continue with a bit more discussion on field trips in the next chapter.

Chapter 11: Day 1 of Your Homeschool

Navigating the First Day of Homeschooling

The first day of homeschooling is a blend of excitement and apprehension. I vividly remember starting my own journey by taking a few pictures of my daughter under a tree. We then retrieved her books from the shelf, and she climbed into her booster seat at the kitchen table. As I opened my teacher's manual, the day transitioned into a formal school experience.

Interestingly, despite the shift to a structured format, our day felt much like any other. We had always enjoyed reading together, and she was familiar with writing and Bible stories from her Awana program. Yet, the first day brought a new sense of novelty and anticipation.

The real challenge began a few weeks in, when the initial excitement waned and the reality of daily schooling set in. My daughter, who preferred playing like her younger sister, began to resist sitting at the table for extended periods. It was a reminder that the first day's enthusiasm might not last, and that homeschooling would require patience.

Whether your first day goes smoothly or presents challenges, it's important to acknowledge your efforts. Allow yourself a well-deserved twenty-minute break at the end of the school day to celebrate the accomplishment of starting something new and outside your comfort zone.

As you embark on each school year, have a plan, but be prepared for deviations. If you find that you needed white glue instead of a glue stick or a textbook didn't arrive on time, remember that your response to these challenges is a part of your children's learning experience. They observe how you handle problems and adapt, which is as valuable as the academic content.

Getting Started That First Day

Make the first day of homeschooling a time for familiarization rather than intense learning. Review the textbooks and teacher's guides, set clear expectations, and introduce the daily schedule in a relaxed manner. Establishing this foundation will help you and your children transition smoothly into the homeschooling routine.

You may feel a range of emotions going from excited to nervous. This is very normal and, honestly, don't we experience that as parents at each step? Understand that your children might not be as excited about the first day of homeschooling as you are. They don't know what school is or, if they are beginning homeschooling after attending a school building, they may have some negative associations with schooling that will take time to heal. Maintain a positive outlook, even if they show reluctance. Consider celebrating the first day with a fun family activity; our family loved to do a movie night or a fire pit with hot dogs and s'mores. These traditions help mark the start of the school year and create lasting memories.

If you've transitioned from a traditional school setting to homeschooling, try to continue any previous first-day traditions.

If this is a new beginning, establish new ones. Ask them about their school day even though you were there. Encourage them to talk about school with other parents or family members, if they like to do that. I had girls and they loved to share about their day. I have heard from some moms of boys that they don't always talk as much about what they did, and that is fine too. At the end of the day, ensure you take time to grade assignments and provide feedback, as immediate responses help address any struggles and reinforce learning. Start to create a routine that is workable to stay on top of planning and assignments. Just as your children will have a routine: Preview, Learn, Review—you will also have your own routine: Teach, Grade, Adjust.

Start your first day at a set time to establish the routine. Prior to the first day, review your supply lists and gather all necessary materials as if your children were attending a traditional school. Inspect the first five days of lessons to ensure you have all the required resources and keep them organized in one place. It can be really stressful to get started on the day and realize you don't have something you need, so the few minutes you take to prepare and make a list will make you feel less stressed and anxious when you're already trying to do things.

To maintain focus, limit the amount of subject material your children work on at a time. Allow for scheduled breaks with scheduled times to restart. For us, we used an egg timer, and I told them exactly how long I was setting the timer for. I tried to allow small five-minute breaks between each subject and a longer ten-to-fifteen-minute break every ninety minutes to two hours when they were younger. As they got older, I actually allowed them to have a bit of self-determination as to when they started. Since we had a DVD curriculum, I also had them do their morning routine and start their school day independently when they were around twelve years old. I wanted them to have the discipline and sense of responsibility to do what was right even when I wasn't hovering over them.

This approach encouraged them to focus during work, knowing there was time to move around, but also take ownership of their own education to the extent they were able at their age. I really believe that because they knew I took it seriously, they took it more seriously. I know you have noticed that I repeat, "Begin on time to set a serious tone for the school day." That is because there were some very difficult times in our life and family when I was focused on emergencies and did not show the same diligence. During those times I noticed that my girls also because much more lax in their attention to school.

The first day is also an opportunity to build essential study skills. While traditional schools may have placed less emphasis on these skills in recent years, homeschooling provides a unique chance to focus on them. Teach your children how to manage their time, organize their work, and review information daily. The first day, even the first week, doesn't have to include their subjects. When my daughters attended private school in high school, the first week was spent getting to know their teachers and classmates, practicing study skills, and doing non-academic lessons. I thought this was a phenomenal way to start the school year. I believe they called it, "Spiritual Enrichment Week." Consider whether you would like to do something like this. If you've already had your first day of school and didn't do this, don't worry. You can build days or weeks like this into your year after a break, or even when you are all feeling a bit burned-out for a change of pace.

Introduce a structured approach to studying and planning. Use tools like journals and planners to teach your children how to track their work and manage their assignments. This practice is beneficial from an early age and helps establish good habits. If you are not strong in this area yourself, we continue to make resources available at DecisionTreeLearning.com to help parent and students.

One fun yet useful practice is to incorporate warm-up exercises to stimulate your children's minds before diving into lessons. Research suggests that short, engaging activities can improve reading comprehension, particularly for children with ADHD. Integrate these exercises into your routine to enhance learning. It doesn't need to be anything more than five minutes of brain teasers, hidden pictures, word searches, or other fun activities to focus the brain on the start of the day.

One word of caution as you get ready for day one. While the difficulties in the family impacted them, I noticed my daughters' attention to their lessons waned when mine did. Our behavior and attitude have a huge influence on our children. Many people criticized me as a homeschooling mom when I started over twenty years ago, so I often felt our family had to be extra focused to overcome the negative homeschooling perceptions. But that was swinging too far the other way and put unnecessary pressure on my kids. Homeschooling should not be an excuse for a lax attitude, but the wrong attitudes of others should not influence how I homeschool my kids.

Remember, while the journey may be challenging, it is also rewarding. Embrace the fun and growth that comes with homeschooling and know that you are capable of making this a successful and enjoyable experience.

Chapter 12: Enriching Homeschooling with Field Trips, Videos, and Real-Life Experiences

Field trips, videos, and excursions offer valuable learning opportunities in a homeschooling environment, often at a fraction of the cost of traditional schools. These activities can be integrated into your homeschool curriculum more frequently, providing a dynamic and engaging learning experience for your children.

Field Trips: Learning Beyond the Homeschool Classroom

Field trips are a fantastic way to bring learning to life. Whether you're visiting an art museum for the joy of experiencing art or exploring a historical site with a specific learning goal in mind, these outings can be tailored to suit your educational objectives.

When planning a field trip, consider what you want your children to gain from the experience. For example, if you're visiting an art museum, think about the focus of your visit. Are you exploring a specific artist, art movement, or time period? Identify key vocabulary, important pieces to observe, and any activities—such as an art scavenger hunt or sketching—that will help reinforce the learning experience. Trips to an apple orchard could include buying a few varieties of apples, picking up leaves on the ground, interviewing the owners, and then reading about the different varieties or history of apples. [Johnny Appleseed comes to mind.]

To make the most of your field trips, consider using journals or worksheets to document observations and reflections. This practice not only enhances learning but also provides a record for review and assessment later on. You can find templates and forms in the appendix of this book or through our supplementary field trip materials available for download.

Field trips don't have to be grand or expensive. Smaller, local museums or parks can be a great outing, but you could also take a larger family vacation to unique locations like the Crater of Diamonds in Arkansas or Mammoth Cave in Kentucky to build a bigger learning experience which can spark curiosity and lead to in-depth projects. For instance, a visit to a natural site could inspire a science project on geology, where your child spends time collecting rocks and later researches their composition and formation.

Videos: A Visual Learning Tool

Videos can be an excellent resource for homeschooling, providing visual and auditory reinforcement of concepts. When using videos, it's important to preview the material and identify key points, vocabulary, and significant events or figures. This preparation allows you to guide your children in focusing on essential aspects of the video.

Some videos, especially educational documentaries, come with ready-made worksheets or study guides. However, if you're using online resources like YouTube, you can create your own by reviewing the video transcripts and identifying key learning points. After watching the video, review the material with your child and incorporate it into their portfolio, making it part of a comprehensive assessment. You could use a current event sheet like this one to help focus your student's review or create a guide yourself.

While films—especially historical fiction—can be engaging, be cautious about their accuracy. Use these films as a tool for developing critical thinking by comparing the portrayal of events in the movie with historical facts. This can be an excellent exercise for older students, helping them to discern fact from fiction and develop a deeper understanding of the subject matter.

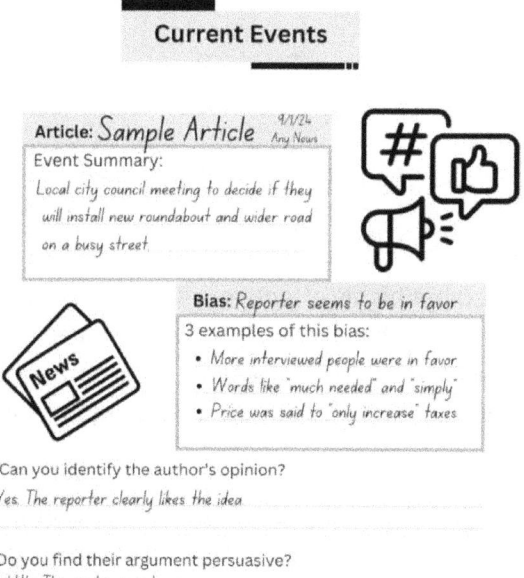

Incorporating Independent Projects in Your Homeschool

Projects are a powerful way for children to demonstrate their understanding and creativity. Whether it's creating a diorama, designing a tartan, or crafting a personal interpretation of a historical artifact, projects allow students to explore topics in a hands-on, meaningful way.

Encourage your children to take ownership of their projects by allowing them to choose topics that interest them. This not only makes learning more enjoyable but also fosters a deeper connection to the material. Projects can be tied to field trips, videos, or other lessons, providing a holistic approach to learning.

Example of Real-Life Learning: The Grocery Store as a Classroom

One often overlooked but highly effective learning experience is a trip to the grocery store. This everyday activity can be transformed into a multi-disciplinary lesson, incorporating math, consumer economics, health and nutrition, and organizational skills.

Before heading to the store, involve your children in planning meals, creating a shopping list, and setting a budget. At the store, they can practice math by calculating costs, comparing prices, and making decisions based on budget constraints. This real-world application of skills is invaluable and can help children understand the practical importance of what they are learning.

After the grocery trip, continue the lesson by organizing the groceries, discussing storage and food safety, and even engaging in cooking together. This process not only reinforces the lessons learned at the store but also teaches important life skills.

As your children move into middle school and high school, this becomes even more important because they need to learn how to manage their time and finances. Explain the time and cost savings of meal planning, involve them more often in meal preparation [as a planned activity, not simply when you are busy], and set a good example by minimizing over-processed foods like take-out and boxed meals.

Enhancing Learning Through Community Resources

Don't forget to explore other community resources, such as libraries and local businesses. Regular trips to the library can teach children how to access and utilize various resources. While most people realize the library offers books, magazines, and movies, our local library offers far more items. Check and see if your library does the same: from books and 3D printers to kitchen appliances and DVD players.

Visits to places like firehouses, local businesses, or even meeting members of the trades like bricklayers, carpenters, and welders can provide insight into different careers and the skills required for various jobs. These excursions can be structured around the Preview, Learn, Review model, where children prepare questions, engage in learning, and then reflect on their experiences afterward.

I have seen homeschoolers shy away from field trips in response to criticism from others who seemed to imply—or say outright—that we didn't take education seriously. But they are very important parts of learning that used to be a regular part of the school year decades ago, and it's something that homeschool parents can offer to their children to enhance their learning in very meaningful ways.

Conclusion

Incorporating field trips, videos, and real-life experiences into your homeschooling routine can make learning more engaging and meaningful for your children. The key is to have clear learning outcomes in mind, involve your children in the process, and tie these activities back to your educational goals.

To support your efforts, I've included ideas to create forms and worksheets at the end of this book, as well as additional resources available for download. Keeping these activities organized and documented will not only enhance your child's learning experience but also provide a valuable portfolio for review and assessment.

Remember, learning is a lifelong journey, and by integrating these diverse experiences into your homeschooling, you're teaching your children that education is not confined to a classroom—it's a part of everyday life.

Chapter 13: Learning to Teach

One of the most important aspects of homeschooling is learning how to teach effectively. This may seem daunting, especially if you don't have a formal teaching background. However, many traditional teachers face similar challenges. While they may learn about educational laws and theories in college, they often aren't adequately trained in breaking down information, identifying learning styles, or managing a classroom effectively. As a homeschooling parent, you can develop these essential teaching skills without attending a traditional teaching school. In fact, much of what is taught in teaching programs may not be directly applicable to your child's learning at home.

I am not saying this to be overly critical of teachers, but to reassure you. I am a woman who homeschooled from kindergarten through 12th grade with multiple children at various learning levels. I do not have a degree in education, but I did a good job. One of my daughters is a math teacher, another writes curriculum, and all four live on their own. I have also worked in both public and private schools. I have seen it from all sides, and I want to assure you: if you are committed to doing this well and getting the skills, you will do it.

The Importance of Writing in Learning

Writing plays a crucial role in the learning process. I strongly advocate incorporating journaling, note-taking, and even cursive writing into your homeschooling curriculum from the early years. Numerous studies suggest a significant connection between the act of writing by hand and the brain's ability to learn and retain information. Unlike typing on a keyboard, the physical act of writing—whether it's jotting down notes, drawing, or solving problems—helps the brain process and remember material more effectively.

Early on, I saw a curriculum that taught cursive beginning in kindergarten as part of literacy. By making the word a single unit of connected characters rather than a string of individual letters, they indicated that the students would be able to retain the word concept. I thought it was a great idea, so I used it with all of my girls.

Beyond penmanship and note-taking, the act of writing for essays and creative writing is so important that one of the key areas I am creating on our website is committed to these areas. So much time is spent online reading content or ideas. We need to be able to identify the bias of the author, what they're trying to get us to believe, and how to form and articulate our own thoughts about everything from understanding the scientific method to systems of government to home maintenance.

While I am a big fan of efficiency, I also know that all great innovations come from a strong understanding of the basics. In your homeschool, take the time to teach the basics.

Engaging Multiple Senses

Engaging multiple senses in the learning process can enhance retention. For example, when my husband and I were in college, we used specific scents or foods, like peppermints, while studying. The idea was that when we encountered these scents or flavors again during an exam, they would help trigger the memory of what we studied. This might sound like a psychological trick, but it worked for us, and it might be a useful tool for your homeschool as well.

A funny story from our own family about this idea—our daughter was so influenced by the practice that when she was in high school attending a private school, her research project for science class was on this very idea. She studied the impact of eating a peppermint on the ability to catch a ball. To rule out the idea that it was simply sugar, some participants were given a sweet candy and others were given peppermints [which contained peppermint oil, not just a flavoring]. Her small sample size of students found decisively for the peppermint improving their ability. And her projects also showed the influence of homeschooling and parent behavior on her in life. She is the same daughter who now writes educational curriculum and, you will not be surprised to learn, it has lots of project-based activities.

Improving Your Long-Term Learning with Journals and Notes

It's also essential to encourage your children to write down notes, steps in solving math problems, reflections on their readings, or any other relevant information. This practice reinforces learning and improves long-term memory. Don't get caught up in the latest educational theories. Instead, focus on practical strategies such as practicing, reviewing, and patient repetition of facts. As you teach, sit with your children, write things out in front of them, and guide them through the process step by step. This method, though simple, is highly effective.

I have tips throughout this book, but I have also created a student study guide that provides an organized space to keep these notes as well as lessons for study skills.

Solutions for the Challenges of Modern Learning and Why They Are Important

Teaching children today can be more challenging due to the distractions of technology. Kids are accustomed to constant entertainment, which can make traditional learning feel boring. However, it's essential to understand that education is not about entertainment. While incorporating technology occasionally to make learning more engaging is fine, the core of education should be about interaction with the material and going deeper into subjects. Encourage your children to focus, even when the learning process isn't flashy or exciting. Depth of understanding comes from persistence, not from constant entertainment.

In fact, I have done a great deal of research on how lessons are structured as part of my preparation for this book, my own teaching, and for my YouTube channels. There is now an emphasis on shifting a camera angle every few seconds, teasing about coming information rather than presenting it in a logical progression, and lots of movement to keep you engaged.

The problem with this is there has also been a great deal of research into the brain and memory which indicates that, for the brain, this is the opposite of what should be done. Things should be broken down and mastered and built up. Jumping from one thing to another, constant movement, and flash startles the brain; they draw attention away from the material, not toward it. If you would like more information on this topic, I suggest the book *Moonwalking with Einstein*. But while I discourage flash, I do understand learning styles and the importance of teaching in a way students can learn.

Learning Styles: Tailoring Education to Your Child

Understanding your child's learning style is crucial. The three primary learning styles are visual, auditory, and kinesthetic. Visual learners benefit from seeing information, such as through pictures, videos, or reading. Auditory learners prefer to hear information: listening to lectures, discussions, or even listening to music while studying is more effective for them. Kinesthetic learners learn best by doing—through hands-on activities, drawing, or building models. Many of these learners also enjoy jobs that require them to use their hands on the job—although not all.

Incorporate your child's learning style into their lessons, but also challenge them to use other styles during the review phase. This approach helps them become more adaptable learners. For instance, if your child learns best visually, encourage them to listen to audio materials or engage in hands-on activities as part of their review process. This way, they gain exposure to different learning methods, which can deepen their understanding. It also helps them to learn and retain information when material isn't presented to them in the way that is easiest for them.

We all know that in life, situations aren't always ideal. Therefore, presenting challenges is also a part of the learning process. As your child gets closer to finishing homeschooling, you might want to begin to present in your preferred style and make part of their learning process modifying and reviewing by redoing the lesson in their own learning style. This is a useful skill that all homeschool parents should build in.

Embracing Mistakes as Part of Learning

Mistakes are a natural and valuable part of the learning process. In traditional schools, there is often little room for mistakes due to the structure of assessments. However, as a homeschooling parent, you have the flexibility to allow your children to make mistakes and learn from them. Encourage them to keep a journal where they can record what worked, what didn't, and why. This reflective practice helps them develop problem-solving skills and resilience.

This is a major part of the projects in the homeschool structure I suggest. We want them to actively test their ideas to find out if they work or not, rather than us giving them the answers. This can be done from preschool on up, always asking questions like:

- Is that the expected result?
- Is that the result we wanted?
- Why did that happen?
- What do we want to try next?

This changes the idea of unexpected results to a learning opportunity and a chance for critical thinking rather than a "wrong answer." Now, there are cases where an answer is clearly wrong, but by framing intellectual curiosity and discovery as a process of successes and learning opportunities, we don't shut down learning.

The Value of Quiet Time and Deep Learning

Deep learning and quiet time are often overlooked in today's fast-paced educational environment. However, they are essential for true understanding and innovation. Like baking bread, where the dough needs time to rest, your child's brain needs quiet time to process and integrate new information. Encourage regular periods of quiet reflection in your homeschooling schedule. This practice allows your children to think deeply about what they've learned, leading to better retention and creative problem-solving. To be clear, these periods are not times for video games or other entertainment. This is actual time where they're permitted to be bored without a stimulus. The ability to process the information without being addicted to the need for constant data and input will help them.

Utilizing Resources and Learning from Others

There are many resources available to support your homeschooling journey. Learning from other experienced teachers can be incredibly valuable. Whether from books, podcasts, or educational websites, don't hesitate to incorporate tried-and-true teaching methods into your curriculum. While it's important to have a budget and not feel pressured to buy every resource available, investing in quality materials that align with your teaching goals is a wise use of your time and money.

When I was a homeschooler, I was often on a very tight budget, so I understand that pressure well. Some of the tools I've created are there to help homeschooling parents organize their various resources in a single place, so that they don't have to waste time trying to find things. That can lead to frustration and a reluctance to use some of the great materials available. Your life will be much easier in your homeschool when you learn how to best organize your specific homeschool. Just like I suggested with working with your own children, journaling and making notes of what worked and what didn't is a great way to do that. If you have the homeschool teacher planner I created, there is a place for that. If not, have a central place to write notes and reflections on what works and what doesn't in your homeschool.

Conclusion: Teaching Your Children How to Learn

The key to successful homeschooling is teaching your children how to learn. As you progress through the chapters in this book, you'll see this theme repeated. Teaching your children to think critically, adapt, and problem-solve will serve them well throughout their lives. They may not remember every fact, but the skills they develop in learning how to learn will be invaluable.

As a homeschooling parent, you don't need a teaching degree to be effective. Focus on the results—are your children learning, grasping information, and able to use it? That's the true measure of your success as their teacher.

Chapter 14: Assessments and Figuring Out If They Are Learning

Assessing your child's learning is a key aspect of homeschooling, and it's one of the areas where homeschooling truly shines compared to traditional education. The beauty of assessments in a homeschool setting is the flexibility and variety you have in evaluating your child's understanding and progress. Unlike conventional schools, where tests and quizzes are the primary tools for assessment, homeschooling allows you to explore various methods that cater to your child's unique learning style.

Types of Assessments Based on What Is Being Assessed

Assessments aren't limited to just tests and quizzes; they can take many forms, each revealing different aspects of learning. For instance, rubrics are excellent for evaluating projects. If your child is working on a project about the Norman Invasion, you can assess their understanding through a combination of essays, research, and videos, all guided by a clear rubric that outlines expectations. This method not only helps you evaluate their knowledge but also gives your child a structured way to demonstrate mastery of the subject.

When it comes to memorizing facts, such as dates or names, flashcards are an effective study tool. Handwritten flashcards, in particular, help reinforce the connection between hand and brain, aiding memory retention. Quizzes and tests, including fill-in-the-blank or multiple-choice questions, are also great for assessing factual knowledge. These methods allow you to see if your child has mastered the basic facts before moving on to more complex tasks.

For synthesis of information and critical thinking, essays are invaluable. Writing an essay requires your child to not only recall facts but also understand and apply them within a broader context. If you want to assess their comprehension of historical dates, for example, using a timeline or fill-in-the-blank exercises can be effective. However, for deeper critical thinking, an essay will provide more insight into their understanding.

In the next chapter, I will show how a rubric can be used in many kinds of projects —to guide project creation, to help your students understand what is required, and to show what a great assignment looks like.

The Importance of Assessment

Assessment is not merely about assigning a grade or proving that your child knows something. It's about ensuring that they understand why this knowledge is important. For example, understanding historical dates is not just about memorization; it's about placing events in context, which helps in understanding the flow of history. Having a clear understanding of why they are learning something truly helps them learn. That means you also need to be clear why you are teaching it, so if there is a topic you don't seem to understand the purpose of, take time to consider the *why*. This is a leadership skill taught to top executives and one that helps with execution. Make sure you're clear on the value of the thing being learned, articulate that to your child, and then assess their understanding—of the facts *and* the relevance.

In homeschooling, assessment also serves to teach transferable skills. For instance, in English, when your child reads a story, they learn about author bias, cultural influence, character development, tone, and plot. These skills are crucial because we receive so much information through written communication; being able to evaluate the bias of the author is essential in discerning the reliability of that information. That is the *why*.

In social studies, learning from historical patterns and cultural influences helps develop a broader understanding of the world. Science, with its emphasis on the scientific method, not only teaches facts but also exposes your child to the process of inquiry, which is fundamental in developing a scientific mindset. Even math, often seen as a subject of rote memorization, is about problem-solving and applying learned processes to real-world situations. That is why we learn them. You may not use a specific equation you learned in math, but the ability to figure out a problem is based in the math story problem which you will do often when you grow up and it is the *why* behind learning the quadratic equation.

Moving Beyond Right and Wrong

One of the key shifts in homeschooling assessment is moving away from a simple right or wrong answer approach. While facts are important, the process of getting to the answer is just as crucial. For example, in math, if your child makes a mistake, it's important to look at the process they followed. Did they understand the problem? Did they apply the correct method? By focusing on the process, you help your child develop critical thinking skills and a deeper understanding of the material.

This approach to assessment encourages a growth mindset. It's not about getting everything right the first time, but about learning from mistakes and improving over time. This is particularly important in subjects like math, where the process of problem-solving is as valuable as the solution itself.

While facts are important, the process of getting to the answer is just as crucial. For example, in math, if your child makes a mistake, it's important to look at the process they followed. Did they understand the problem? Did they apply the correct method? By focusing on the process, you help your child develop critical thinking skills and a deeper understanding of the material.

This approach to assessment encourages a growth mindset. It's not about getting everything right the first time, but about learning from mistakes and improving over time.

Critical Thinking vs. Criticism Thinking

As you assess your child's learning, it's important to distinguish between critical thinking and criticism thinking. Critical thinking involves evaluating information, questioning assumptions, and considering different perspectives to arrive at a reasoned conclusion. It's about examining whether the expected outcome aligns with the initial assumptions and, if not, figuring out why.

On the other hand, criticism thinking is about finding faults without constructive analysis. It's common in social media and some academic environments, where the focus is on tearing down ideas rather than understanding them. In homeschooling, fostering critical thinking is essential because it teaches your child to approach problems thoughtfully and systematically, rather than simply pointing out what's wrong.

Practical Application in Homeschooling

When assessing your child's progress, remember that it's not just about whether they got the answer right, but about understanding their thought process. Did they use the right tools and strategies? If they struggled, was it because they didn't understand the question, or did they use the wrong method? This reflective approach to assessment helps you guide your child more effectively, identifying areas where they need more support or different strategies.

It's also important to recognize your child's natural strengths and challenges. Not every child will excel in every subject, and that's okay. The goal of homeschool assessments should be to help your child reach a satisfactory level of understanding in all areas, while also allowing them to excel in subjects they are passionate about. For example, your child might not need to master advanced math if they're not pursuing a career that requires it. However, they should still be capable of handling basic math necessary for everyday life.

Encouraging Effort and Resilience

As you guide your child through their education, encourage them to try new things, even if they are difficult. Failure is a natural part of the learning process, and it's important for your child to learn that not getting an A on everything is okay. It's the effort and the learning that count.

Assessments in homeschooling should be about understanding and growth, not just about grades. By focusing on the process, fostering critical thinking, and recognizing individual strengths and weaknesses, you can ensure that your child is truly learning and developing the skills they need for the future.

Chapter 15: Rubrics and How They Actually Teach Your Kids How to Learn

The Power of Rubrics in Homeschooling

Rubrics are often seen as intimidating or complex, yet they are incredibly valuable tools for teaching children how to approach larger assignments or projects. More than just a grading tool, a rubric provides a clear framework that encourages self-determination and helps students develop critical thinking skills.

Understanding the Role of Rubrics

A rubric clearly outlines the expectations for an assignment and defines the criteria for each section. As a homeschooling parent, creating and using rubrics can help your child grasp the nuances between mediocre and excellent work. Many students often wonder why they didn't receive an A despite following the instructions. The answer lies in understanding that a C represents meeting expectations, a B exceeds them, and an A signifies exceptional work.

In today's world, where participation trophies are common and marketing slogans tell us we deserve everything we want, it's crucial to challenge our children. Doing so equips them with the skills necessary to excel beyond graduation. A rubric is an excellent tool for this purpose because it clearly shows what each level requires and, depending on how specific or nuanced you make it, the student can start to gain understanding of how one goes about bringing their work to a higher level.

Components of an Effective Rubric

To illustrate the effectiveness of rubrics, I've created examples for five different grade levels, which you can adapt to suit your needs. These rubrics evaluate criteria such as:

- Identifying the problem
- Determining who is affected by the problem
- Proposing solutions
- Considering the impact if no solution is implemented
- Evaluating the impact if a solution is implemented

These elements encourage students to think critically about the issues at hand, whether they are writing an essay, completing a project, or engaging in a debate. In case you don't have extensive experience being graded with rubrics, or you want to see better how they help your child learn, I have created an example below.

Example: The Sidewalk Dilemma

Let's explore a simple yet impactful example: installing a sidewalk.

1. **Identifying the Problem:** The issue is that a heavily trafficked area lacks a sidewalk, forcing pedestrians to walk on private property or in the road, which is unsafe.

2. **Who Is Affected**: Pedestrians, drivers, and property owners are all impacted by the lack of a sidewalk.

3. **Possible Solutions**: Solutions might include installing a sidewalk on one side of the road, creating a pedestrian path adjacent to the road, or constructing barriers to separate pedestrians from vehicles.

4. **Impact of No Solution**: If no action is taken, the safety of pedestrians remains compromised, and property owners may face continued issues with foot traffic on their lawns.

5. **Impact of a Solution**: Installing a sidewalk may involve costs, disruptions to traffic during construction, and potential loss of property for homeowners, but it would enhance pedestrian safety and community connectivity.

By breaking down the problem into these components, students learn to analyze a seemingly simple issue from multiple perspectives. A rubric for this exercise might allocate points based on how clearly the problem is identified, the depth of understanding shown, and the quality of the proposed solutions.

Encouraging Critical Thinking with Rubrics

When students receive feedback based on a rubric, they can see where they excelled and where they fell short. For example, if a student receives fewer points for problem identification, they can revisit their work to deepen their analysis. This process teaches them to think more critically, consider different perspectives, and articulate their thoughts clearly.

Rubrics can also be tailored to encourage specific types of thinking. For instance, you might adjust the rubric to place more weight on the solution identification section if that aligns with your educational goals. Alternatively, you could use a rubric to teach students about bias by evaluating current events articles and analyzing the presence of bias based on specific criteria.

Involving Students in Rubric Creation

For older students, such as those in 4th or 5th grade, consider involving them in the creation of the rubric. This exercise fosters critical thinking as they decide what criteria should be evaluated and how much weight each criterion should carry. They learn to articulate their reasoning and understand the subjective nature of evaluations.

For example, when identifying a problem, the rubric might specify that students need to provide a minimum of three supporting examples. This requirement not only ensures clarity but also teaches students to support their arguments with evidence.

The Lasting Value of Rubrics

While rubrics are not applicable to every assignment, they are a powerful tool when used consistently. Over time, your child will internalize the rubric's expectations, learning to think multidimensionally about problems, evaluate arguments, and draw conclusions based on available data. This approach nurtures critical thinking skills from a young age, setting the foundation for lifelong learning.

In the back of this book, you will find several example rubrics for different grade levels. You can adapt these rubrics based on your child's needs and educational goals. Additionally, my other book, *Your Homeschool* Blueprint*: Deciding, Organizing, and Teaching at Home*, available for purchase, includes worksheets and tools designed to help homeschooling parents effectively implement rubrics in their teaching.

Rubrics are more than just grading tools—they are essential components in fostering thoughtful, independent learners.

Chapter 16: *This Isn't What I Thought It Would Be*—Some of the Daily Challenges and Realities of Homeschooling

Homeschooling, while deeply rewarding, comes with its own unique set of challenges that can sometimes be daunting even for the most dedicated parents. It is vital to approach these challenges with honesty and openness, recognizing that they are not indicators of failure, but part of the homeschooling journey.

Everyday Struggles

Being a homeschool parent is akin to any other form of parenting—filled with love, dedication, and occasional frustrations. Like any parent, homeschoolers want what's best for their children, which means navigating through both good and bad days. Challenges such as lack of enthusiasm from children, the pressure to be the "perfect" teacher, and balancing the dual roles of parent and educator are common. Children might question the need for schooling on a seemingly perfect day for a break, echoing the sentiments of "Why do we have school today when others don't?" or "I'm bored." These expressions can be tough to handle as they often feel like a reflection on our teaching.

Technological Challenges

In today's digital age, another significant challenge is managing technology use. Keeping devices like cell phones and tablets in common areas is crucial, not only to shield children from potential online threats but also to foster accountability and safe browsing habits. This practice also helps in maintaining focus during school hours and ensures that technology supports rather than hinders educational goals.

Emotional and Physical Exhaustion for the Homeschooling Parent

Homeschooling can be physically and emotionally draining. The feeling of isolation, the blurring lines between work and home life, and the constant visibility of unfinished tasks can overwhelm even the most organized parent. It's essential to find small escapes or moments of respite, whether it's a brief outing or simply a few minutes alone, to recharge and maintain perspective.

Also, I want you to know as a homeschool mom, we are all experiencing it, even when we don't talk about it. It is draining and it is hard. We are often trying to homeschool feeling like we don't have all of the resources we would like to have, or we feel like we aren't doing enough to help our kids learn. I often wished I could go somewhere and be "Tiffany" rather than "Mom" for a while. But I heard someone describe the homeschool life like this: "The days were long, but the years were short." Each year as I got ready to start school with them again, I was excited and nervous. I also stood in awe of how much time had already passed.

Even with that, I readily admit that I did not prioritize breaks for myself and that made me a less effective homeschooling parent than I could have been. I regret that choice and that is honestly one of the reasons I wrote this book.

Navigating Child Resistance and Diverse Interests

It is not uncommon for children to resist lessons or particular subjects. This resistance, however, should not be seen as a reflection of parental inadequacy but rather as a natural part of a child's educational journey. Each child has unique interests, and as a homeschooling parent, you are sometimes tasked with teaching things they don't enjoy. Try not to take it personally. Work to maintain enthusiasm and commitment, recognizing that interests can diverge, which is perfectly acceptable, but don't give in to skipping things they don't enjoy to make things easier.

Conclusion

The path of homeschooling is strewn with challenges that test patience, resilience, and creativity. However, these challenges also present opportunities for growth, learning, and deeper family connections. By acknowledging and preparing for these realities, homeschooling parents can foster a supportive and enriching environment that benefits both the child and the educator. While the journey may be demanding, the outcomes—educated, well-rounded children—are profoundly gratifying.

Chapter 17: Will My Kids Be Able to Get a Good Job? What About College?

A common concern for parents who homeschool, or who are considering homeschooling, is whether their children will be able to secure a good job in the future. This question is entirely valid, as preparing kids for adulthood includes equipping them for successful careers.

The short answer is yes—homeschoolers can certainly achieve rewarding employment. Many universities and employers actively seek out homeschooled students, and I witnessed this firsthand when my own children were nearing graduation. However, let's delve deeper into this issue, because it does require work and preparation on the part of the homeschooling parent.

Early Years: Focus on Learning Fundamentals

If you are just starting your homeschooling journey with young children, such as those in kindergarten, it's important not to be overly concerned about their future careers at this stage. Early education should focus on teaching children the basics—math, reading, penmanship, and foundational skills. The emphasis should be on cultivating a love for learning rather than fixating on career outcomes.

At this stage, consider things like a career day or taking time to help introduce your children to the jobs people have in the community. This can be as formal as scheduling appointments to visit someone at work or as informal as explaining when you are on errands that the people helping you are at work and asking that person about their job. When I was in elementary school every year, we had career day and each of us got a chance to see three or four people of our choice talk about their job. If you aren't able to do that, then find out what jobs they like and see if you can find videos on it.

Transitioning to Middle School: Planning for the Future

As children approach the end of primary school and enter middle school, it becomes more pertinent to consider their future career paths. This is the time to start thinking about long-term goals and how to support your child's aspirations.

Ask yourself:

- What does a "good job" mean to your child?
- Are they interested in a job that will require specialized training? If so, what should they do in school to be ready for those programs?

Explore local opportunities relevant to their interests. For instance, if your child is interested in firefighting, look into local volunteer fire departments or fire schools to understand the requirements and opportunities available. If they are interested in business, are there opportunities in local businesses or retail establishments? Check into after-school clubs in your community or county vocational programs.

High School and Beyond: Tailoring Education for Career Goals

When your child reaches high school, consider the following options to enhance their career prospects:

1. **College Track**: Look into online college courses or dual-enrollment programs if your state offers them. These can provide college credits while still in high school, demonstrating their ability to succeed in higher education and improving their future opportunities.

2. **Vocational Training and Apprenticeships**: Research local vocational programs or apprenticeship opportunities. Practical experience in a field of interest can be invaluable. See what the application process is and any specific pre-requisite learning they need to qualify.

3. **Hybrid Homeschooling Programs**: If you are concerned about academic transcripts or your ability to teach higher level STEM topics, you can consider enrolling your child in a homeschooling program affiliated with a local private school. These programs often maintain official transcripts and records, which can be beneficial for college applications or job placements. They also allow your child to participate in extracurriculars and a class or two for an additional fee.

4. **Portfolios and Documentation**: Maintain a portfolio of your child's work and assessments. This can include samples of their best work, notes, and any standardized grading rubrics used. A well-documented portfolio supports the grades you assign and can be useful for college applications or job searches.

Exploring Opportunities

Encourage your child to engage in job shadowing and local programs related to their interests. This hands-on exploration can help them make informed decisions about their future careers.

Investigate resources available to homeschooling families. Some states offer vouchers for textbooks and resources, or reduced-price college courses. Understanding and utilizing these resources can further support your child's education and career preparation.

If your state does not have these programs, or you don't qualify, many private colleges allow high school students to take college classes with dual enrollment for a reduced tuition rate. These can be a bit expensive, but they are substantially less expensive than the full tuition rate and it is for dual high school and college credit.

Embracing the Homeschool Advantage

Many homeschooled students have unique opportunities to explore diverse interests and gain practical experience that may not be as readily available in traditional school settings. From my experience as a homeschooling parent, as well as having children in public and private schools, I believe that any child can succeed with the right support and tools. It's our role as parents to provide the best resources and guidance to help our children achieve their goals. It is up to our children to take advantage of these opportunities to create the best future possible. Understand that what you do is very important, but nothing guarantees a specific outcome. I put so much pressure on myself as a homeschool parent because I felt it was up to me to ensure my children were successful. My role was to provide a great learning environment. My daughters created their future.

In summary, preparing homeschooled children for a successful career involves thoughtful planning and resourcefulness, but there are definite advantages. Find out about deadlines, try to make opportunities for your children to find out about various kinds of jobs, and be sure you've found out about requirements for various programs. Your children will likely change their mind multiple times, but it is simply another opportunity for them to find out about other career options.

By focusing on their interests, exploring available opportunities, and maintaining thorough documentation, you can help your child build a strong foundation for their future.

Chapter 18: When Do I Stop Homeschooling?

When I started looking at homeschooling, my plan was to homeschool the entire way through; but many parents choose to do it for a shorter period of time from the outset for a myriad of reasons. The most common scenario I saw when I was homeschooling was to homeschool through elementary school, and then introduce the child to a school building in middle school/junior high.

This was typically because the teacher-parents felt they could sufficiently teach the lower grades but wanted their children to attend classes when the subjects were more difficult or specialized. Around the early 2020s, I saw this trend changing, with research indicating the majority of homeschooled children were middle school age.

Some reasons that I've heard people say they stopped homeschooling in high school was for the access to extracurriculars, career preparation, and socialization. I think there is also an intimidation factor for parents whose children want to go to college. While colleges actively recruit homeschooled students, what about scholarships? I am not sure of the answer, and I personally think it is this fear of missing out on free money that makes parents shift gears in high school.

Whatever you decide to do, deciding to stop homeschooling should be done with the transition in mind.

Contact the school the school year before planned enrollment so you can find out what your student needs to know/do to be adequately prepared.

Take tests to find holes and fill them. While this should be done periodically anyway, misalignment with the new school's curriculum can cause huge problems with the transition. We experienced this with our daughters when they entered the school building for the first time. Things were taught in a different order, so they had to quickly try to learn the material they didn't know, and then suffer through re-learning material they had already mastered. I also experienced this in high school when I moved to a new school district between 9th and 10th grade. It took more than a year of tons of studying and tutoring to stabilize my math grades.

My parents didn't have the ability to help me transition between schools in two different states. As a homeschooling parent, you do. So take advantage of that flexibility.

Try to learn as much as possible about the structure of the classrooms. If your children have always been homeschooled, the unfamiliar structure and expectations can be difficult to navigate. Start to build in structures similar to the new school to aid that change.

If possible, particularly if there is not a normal school change when they enter [like in 4th grade, 7th grade, 10th grade where there's no logical break] see if there is a hybrid schooling option, so the child can begin the school part-time before jumping in fully. This worked for my oldest daughter when she did hybrid school in 10th grade and then went to school full time in 11th and 12th grades.

Even if you homeschool through the end of high school, you should make the last two years about working on the transition after graduation and take whatever opportunity you can to provide your student the information and time to prepare themselves.

But understand, your child may choose not to use these opportunities to prepare. If they do that, the logical end is that they will have more stress, etc. This is a part of life and a natural consequence.

You shouldn't homeschool because you want to be a "helicopter" or "lawnmower" parent. You shouldn't do it to try to micromanage your child. You should be working to provide the best opportunity for your child to learn—and that also means learning through natural consequences. Don't use your homeschool to create unrealistic expectations of life, but to allow them the best possible chance of navigating life on their own.

Preparation for Life

I cannot tell you when you should stop homeschooling any more than I can tell you when to start, but I can tell you some considerations that went into our very difficult decision to stop homeschooling.

- I found a job outside of the home. It was part-time, but it made it harder for me to homeschool because of the commute and schedule.

- My oldest wanted to apply for scholarships and the program she was initially looking at was not homeschooler friendly. We moved to a hybrid model, and I got to know a few of the teachers and liked their teaching philosophy.

- All three of my homeschoolers were at a natural transition point.

But I do have some regrets about ending homeschooling when I did. The financial strain of the hybrid program introduced other problems. My kids were immediately introduced to bullying that I never expected, and the very small size of the school severely limited their course options. Since we lived on the state line and my kids were not living in the same state as their new private school, there were many things they were not legally allowed to participate in—for example, sports—which further cemented their feeling like outsiders at times.

Two of the three said that if they could, they would have homeschooled all the way to graduation, but also didn't regret going to the school building.

The decision to homeschool the whole way through shifting to moving them to a school building happened over the course of six months, so I am saying that you don't have to necessarily worry about it as you are looking at your first year of homeschooling. If you are entering homeschooling planning to end before graduation, I would urge you to find out now what your children will need to have mastered to be fully prepared to enter that new school. Don't just adjust academically, but also start to move the structure of your school day the last two years to resemble the bell schedule, etc. of the new building to make it easier for them to adjust.

Chapter 19: Preparing Your Child for Life Beyond Your Homeschool

In this chapter, we delve into preparing your child for life beyond the homeschool environment. While we have touched on this subject in various other chapters, this section is designed for parents who wish to explore these topics more thoroughly or who are homeschooling older children.

The Importance of Life Skills

Preparing a child for adulthood encompasses more than just academic knowledge. While a solid foundation in academic subjects is crucial, integrating life skills into your homeschooling curriculum is equally important. Life skills cover a broad spectrum of practical abilities necessary for independent living. You are certainly teaching these as part of being a good parent, but these are also overlooked, yet useful, academic topics for your homeschool. These include:

1. **Basic Household Management:** Teach your child how to make a grocery list, cook simple meals, manage laundry, and handle basic stain removal. Familiarize them with reading recipes, paying bills, and balancing a checkbook. Even in an era where physical checkbooks are less common, understanding how to write a check remains a valuable skill.

2. **Understanding Utilities and Expenses:** Introduce your child to the concepts of paying for utilities such as electricity, internet, gas, water, and sewer. Discuss the financial responsibilities associated with renting or buying a property and explain the differences between these options.

3. **Automobile Ownership or Using Public Transportation**: This can include topics on costs associated with automobile ownership or using public transportation. Discuss auto clubs and how to evaluate their value and whether you should have one or not. One thing often overlooked when deciding where to live is the cost of auto insurance, which can vary wildly from state to state or even major cities. In places like New York, Chicago, and other larger cities, the cost of parking is a very real consideration and can make automobile ownership impossible, so teaching them how to research these kinds of costs is useful in your homeschool and can even be a reasonable math lesson.

4. **Understanding Housing**: Teach your child how to evaluate rental properties or potential homes for purchase. Discuss finding roommates, managing interpersonal relationships, and recognizing potential hazards.

5. **Budgeting**: A fundamental life skill, budgeting involves planning where money will be spent, how much will be allocated, and how much should be saved. This includes understanding taxes, renewing auto tags, and managing insurance. Emphasize the importance of tracking spending to avoid overspending and to make necessary adjustments. Budgeting is *not* simply tracking where your money goes. That is bookkeeping. When you have a 1. , you need to create a plan for spending and then evaluate if that plan is being followed. Make sure your child understands the difference.

We began teaching our kids budgeting in elementary school; by the time they entered high school, they received a weekly allowance [at the time it was $20/week, now it would probably be $30-$40], and we paid no expenses for them beyond regular groceries and medical expenses. If they needed clothes, they bought them. If they had a birthday party to attend, they paid.

I didn't simply give them that much money and tell them to "go have fun." I taught them, using the budgeting tools I've created [available at DecisionTreeLearning.com], how to anticipate what expenses they had coming up, how to save for expenses like back-to-school shopping or the holidays, and other skills.

They also were required to help at the house for the money but could also earn additional income by doing certain things around the house for a set fee. They were obligated to complete these tasks and if they were going to be gone, they had to see that it was covered [often by paying a sibling to do it], or they had money deducted. We were able to do this because we began teaching these skills in our homeschool.

Allow your child to make financial decisions and learn from their mistakes while they are still at home. This helps them build resilience and prepares them for the larger financial responsibilities of adulthood. Simulate real-life scenarios to help them understand the consequences of their choices.

6. **Credit Management**: Educate your child about the responsible use of credit. Using credit cards wisely—such as paying off balances monthly and leveraging rewards—can be beneficial. Understanding different perspectives on debt and credit use is also crucial.

Incorporating Life Skills into High School Education

For high school students, consider making life skills a part of their elective courses. These skills can be integrated alongside volunteer work, which is often a graduation requirement in many school districts. Including life skills in the curriculum prepares students for practical aspects of adulthood such as job readiness and financial independence.

Assessment wouldn't be grading on how well they did—because they will make mistakes, and the financial ramifications will be a better teacher—but rather have them journal on lessons and share insights they've learned. This is where a grading rubric would be particularly helpful. You would want to create one that focuses on the lessons you want them to learn, not the outcome you want them to achieve.

It can be difficult to grade someone on cooking skills or how well they fold clothing. Also, there isn't a right or wrong choice when deciding on things like apartments, insurance, or job selection. That is why it is important to think about what your goals are for the lessons, the learning outcomes, the skills you want to encourage, and how you'll evaluate if they have accomplished this. We have created resources to help parents [and will continue to do so] at DecisionTreeLearning.com

Financial literacy takes time, so giving them a grade based on saving a certain amount of money will be far less useful than them journaling and understanding how lack of planning impacted their ability to do or have what they needed or wanted. Rewarding the reflection, not the outcome, will create long-term skills and your grading should encourage the behavior you try to develop—not just reward or punish a specific outcome. [For more on that look at the chapter on assessment.]

Career Exploration and Vocational Training

Not all students will pursue college after high school, nor is it the best path for everyone. Vocational training can be highly beneficial. For instance, my husband, who was dedicated to becoming a firefighter paramedic, started his vocational training right after high school. He engaged in job shadowing and explored his career options early on, which guided his educational and professional choices. After almost a decade as a paramedic, he decided to return to school to become a nurse, but he was able to use his job as a paramedic to keep paying bills while he pursued that goal. Vocational training for the win!

Encourage your child to explore various career options and vocational programs. Whether they are interested in skilled trades or other vocations, early exposure to these fields can help them make informed decisions about their future. If you continue homeschooling into later grades, consult with school guidance counselors or explore local programs to understand available opportunities.

Encouraging Independence in Your Older Homeschooler

It is a common misconception that parents homeschool their children in order to prevent them from growing up—at least it was when I was homeschooling. The truth is that I've seen many homeschooling families using their homeschool to foster significant independence. In fact, there was a study done in 2014 by Albert Cheng and published in a peer reviewed journal that found that homeschoolers were more tolerant than public-schooled students when it came to engaging with people of other opinions. I have put the link at the end of this chapter as well as a 2022 study that found additional findings that reinforced the Cheng research. Rather than shielding our children, we give them a very firmly grounded understanding of why we believe what we believe, and we teach our kids to do the same. That doesn't mean that, universally, homeschoolers will behave a particular way any more than public-schooled children or private-schooled children. What it means is that someone who feels secure in who they are and where they come from will often feel more confident and comfortable and will thus be more independent.

Conclusion

Preparing your child for life beyond homeschooling requires more than just academic readiness. It involves equipping them with essential life skills such as managing a household, navigating job applications, understanding financial responsibilities, and making informed decisions about their future. By integrating these skills into your homeschooling curriculum, you help ensure that your child is well prepared to face the challenges and opportunities of adulthood.

This comprehensive approach to education aligns with the goals of homeschooling: not only to provide academic instruction but also to prepare children for a successful and self-sufficient life.

Does Homeschooling or Private Schooling Promote Political Intolerance? Evidence From a Christian University. Author Albert Cheng

http://dx.doi.org/10.1080/15582159.2014.875411

The Kids are Alright II: Social Engagement in Young Adulthood as a Function of K-12 Schooling Type, Personality Traits, and Parental Education Level.

https://www.nheri.org/the-kids-are-alright-ii-social-engagement-in-young-adulthood-as-a-function-of-k-12-schooling-type-personality-traits-and-parental-education-level/

Chapter 20: Special Considerations

In this section, I will cover a number of special considerations that come up in homeschooling.

Incorporating Bible Classes into Homeschooling

For those who wish to integrate Bible study and scripture memorization into their homeschooling routine, there are several effective approaches to consider. You can discuss scripture, doctrine, practical application, and the Bible as a historical document. Looking at all of them is very useful not only to learn about the foundation of your beliefs or share your beliefs with your kids—so hopefully they'll come and follow behind you—but also to recognize the historical significance of the Bible as a written work that is thousands of years old.

You can read great works from apologists who have information on historical accuracy. That isn't really my area of expertise, so I won't speak extensively on it, but I would encourage you to incorporate those things as well, and I will list a few books on the Decision Tree Learning website that I liked for that purpose to help you get started.

Drawing from years of experience in homeschooling and blending faith with education, I want to offer practical ideas and resources for teaching the Bible both as a foundational text of faith and a significant historical document.

The Bible as a Historical Document

It's essential to recognize that the Bible is not only a cornerstone of faith but also a historical document. During my college years at a secular institution, I studied the Bible as part of ancient literature, which enriched my understanding of its historical context. This perspective is valuable for both educating your children about the Bible's historical significance and reinforcing its role as the foundation of your faith.

Don't be intimidated by the vocabulary and your own limitations; as I said, I'm not an expert either, but we did read books as a family and talk about what they said. This allowed me to learn with my children, which we all really enjoyed. We discovered things together. I really feel this reinforced the idea of lifelong learning to my children.

In addition to reading the Bible and reading about the Bible as a historical document, there is, of course, the very practical application of the Bible to your life. How does it become more than simply a large book? How can it serve as a guide to life decisions? Below I share some key components I used in creating our Bible learning at various ages and stages. This also extended beyond our formalized homeschool time to conversations with my children and my own personal study. Feel free to use this as a full framework or as simply a starting point to your own Bible class.

Key Components of Bible Classes

1. **Scripture Memorization**: Incorporate regular scripture memorization into your Bible classes. This can be done through

monthly or weekly verses or selecting life verses. The Bible encourages us to internalize and discuss scripture regularly. Ensure that memorization is accompanied by a discussion of the context to prevent misinterpretation. You can expand this project into part of penmanship for younger children, art class for all ages, essays for English class, and any other number of classes. Allow your child, if they are interested, to share if they'd like to do a special project around their scripture memorization to encourage more engagement.

2. **Bible Stories**: Dive into a wide range of Bible stories. While well-known stories such as Noah's ark and the fall of Adam and Eve are important, exploring lesser-known figures like Hezekiah or episodes like the Exodus can be equally enriching. Use these stories as a basis for memorization to reinforce the lessons learned. As with scripture memorization, looking at specific people in the Old and New Testaments and viewing their story in the Bible can be a starting point for deeper reflection of life lessons, contemporary history [what was happening elsewhere at the same time], and what we learn about God's nature through what happened.

3. **Application to Life**: Apply the teachings of specific books or scriptures to real-life situations. For instance, the book of Habakkuk was an essential text for me during challenging times. Honestly, I would just read it over and over and look at what the story said, and it would build up my faith. It would also remind me that God knows more than I do and what my response should be to him during times of confusing circumstances. This illustrates how scripture can provide guidance and comfort. Similarly, relate the teachings of books like 1 and 2 Timothy to contemporary life. It is useful if your child is considering going into ministry, or maybe a new pastor has joined your church. There is obviously the book of Proverbs that has wisdom, or Psalms that show the emotions we all experience and the intimacy of God.

4. **Studying Specific Books**: I advocate for reading specific books of the Bible in their entirety. In the New Testament, many books are letters written to early Christian communities. Listening to or reading these letters in one sitting can provide a cohesive understanding of their message. For example, listening to 1 and 2 Corinthians consecutively can offer valuable insights that you don't get by reading a few verses or even a chapter. This works best for books that were written as letters and can be finished in forty-five minutes or less; but even some of the longer books like Isaiah or Jeremiah, or even Daniel, take on a different feel when read straight through. I have experienced this in my own life and reading. Books that I thought were dark and scary because I typically read a particular section over and over took on a completely different tone when I read them in their context from beginning to end.

5. **Doctrine Lessons**: Explore the doctrines of your church and their biblical foundations. If you are part of a denominational church, do the same with the teachings of the denomination. Search out the scriptural foundation of the beliefs. Understand how these doctrines point to Christ and guide behavior. This helps in integrating the teachings of the Bible into daily life and understanding their practical implications. This doesn't have to wait until high school. In our church we do this in the younger elementary grades. We even introduce them to more complex theological terms, but we take the time to break those terms into simple English as well, so that it doesn't seem intimidating to younger children.

6. **Historical and Cultural Context**: Consider the historical and cultural background of the scriptures. This includes understanding the culture in which the Bible was written and how other texts and historical evidence support its content. Tailor this exploration to the child's age and interest level. You can find many books on these topics that didn't exist when I was starting out. I have particularly enjoyed studies that are done by

Messianic Jews [people who are Jewish by culture and bring that insight to the study of the Bible].

Remember This is Enjoyable

Bible classes should be engaging and enjoyable. Approach the classes as you would any other subject—mathematics, art, science, or English. Avoid making these sessions confrontational or stressful. This is something we get to do, and it is a book from our loving, Holy God to show us about Him. It is relational.

> These are the proverbs of Solomon, David's son, king of Israel. Their purpose is to teach people wisdom and discipline, to help them understand the insights of the wise. Their purpose is to teach people to live disciplined and successful lives, to help them do what is right, just, and fair. These proverbs will give insight to the simple, knowledge and discernment to the young. Let the wise listen to these proverbs and become even wiser. Let those with understanding receive guidance by exploring the meaning in these proverbs and parables, the words of the wise and their riddles. Fear of the LORD is the foundation of true knowledge, but fools despise wisdom and discipline. [Proverbs 1:1-7 NLT]

Present Bible study as a critical part of your homeschooling curriculum, equal in importance to other subjects. The Bible's teachings have profound implications and should be integrated into your educational approach with care and respect.

Finally, there may be days that your children are less than enthusiastic about Bible class. Don't take it any more personally than when they do it with other subjects. While Bible class is important, it shouldn't be a point of contention because that will just cause further resistance. Continue to teach on those days just as you would teach other subjects: with a disciplined approach, but not emotional. The Word, unlike the other subjects, grows inside of us as we read it. Allow it to penetrate your heart as well as theirs and give you peace. Let it be a highlight of your homeschool day, not a battleground.

By incorporating these elements into your Bible classes, you can create a well-rounded and meaningful study of scripture that supports both faith and education.

Integrating Vocational Education into Your Homeschooling

Vocational education can be a valuable addition to a homeschooling curriculum, especially as your child approaches high school. To ensure a smooth integration of vocational programs, it is crucial to begin planning well in advance—ideally, three years before your child is expected to participate. This early preparation allows you to familiarize yourself with the requirements and application processes involved in vocational education programs in your area. If you haven't started that early, all is not lost. Begin now.

Early Preparation

Vocational programs often require specific qualifications and forms, which can differ significantly from the standard homeschooling requirements. Unlike public schools, where a team of professionals handles these details, you will need to navigate these requirements independently. Start by researching available programs, which might include after-school or weekend explorer programs, evening apprenticeships, or dual enrollment options. Identifying these opportunities early will help you align them with your homeschooling plan.

Understanding Program Requirements

Each vocational program has its own set of requirements and prerequisites. It is essential to understand how these programs fit into your child's overall education plan. For instance, vocational courses in fields like medical technology may include components that count towards math credits due to their practical applications, such as dosage calculations. Knowing how these programs integrate with high school graduation requirements will help you determine any additional coursework your student might need. It will also allow you to have flexibility in your schooling without creating unnecessary extra burdens for you or your child.

Balancing Vocational Education and Homeschooling

It is important to remember that vocational education does not have to be an additional burden on top of a full homeschooling schedule. Public school students often have dedicated time for online coursework and vocational training; similarly, your homeschooling approach can be adapted to include vocational components without overwhelming your daily routine.

If you choose to incorporate vocational education, you can use your homeschooling flexibility to provide supplementary life skills and additional educational excellence. The goal is to ensure that your child is well-prepared for life beyond high school, both academically and practically.

One piece that could cause additional work that you'll need to account for is transportation. While public school students may have access to off-site training if it is part of a large class program, you will likely have to make travel arrangements yourself which could conflict with schooling other children. This isn't to discourage or dissuade you from doing these programs, but it is a reminder that you will need to be even more disciplined in your planning during these times.

Planning Ahead

Consider exploring vocational programs as early as 8th or 9th grade if you believe this path aligns with your child's interests. Engage with schools and program representatives to gather information and address any questions you may have. Early research and preparation will enable you to make informed decisions and integrate vocational education seamlessly into your homeschooling plan.

By approaching vocational education with a well-thought-out strategy, you can provide your child with valuable skills and experiences while maintaining a balanced and effective homeschooling environment.

College Dual Enrollment Options

Understanding Dual Enrollment

Dual enrollment allows students to take college-level courses while still in high school. These can sometimes be offered at no cost or with a fee, depending on the educational institution and its funding policies. Public school students often have access to such programs, and it is worth exploring whether similar opportunities are available for homeschooled students.

In some cases, like our own experience, the availability of these programs can vary. For instance, because we lived on a state line, our hybrid homeschool [and later, full-time private school] was in a different state. This meant free state dual enrollment options at their school were not available to us and we had to cover the tuition for their dual enrollment. Our local school district was very openly hostile to homeschoolers, and so we did not participate in public-school options that students in other states and counties can take part it.

Your local district may be different, or the laws more inclusive allowing homeschool students to be a part of sports in their public school and other activities. Don't be afraid to investigate these options. I found HSLDA.org [Home School Legal Defense Association] to be a great resource throughout my time homeschooling.

Benefits of Dual Enrollment

Dual enrollment can be highly advantageous. It enables students to earn college credits while completing high school and can even reduce the time and cost of a college degree. For example, my son-in-law graduated high school with nearly an associate's degree due to his extensive participation in dual enrollment courses. His courses were paid for by the state and were in lieu of his high school coursework. This approach is particularly effective for students who spend their final year or even the last year and a half of high school focusing primarily on college coursework.

This flexibility not only prepares students for college but also opens doors to other educational opportunities and programs that may have specific prerequisites. Even if a student does not choose to continue with higher education immediately, the college credits earned can be beneficial for future academic or vocational pursuits.

How Dual Enrollment Works

In a dual enrollment program, students might take courses that fulfill high school requirements while simultaneously earning college credit. For instance, rather than taking a standard high school English class, a student could enroll in a college-level Shakespearean literature course. This arrangement ensures that the student meets both high school graduation requirements and accumulates college credits.

However, it is important to consider that college grades earned through dual enrollment will impact the student's academic record. Poor performance in these courses can negatively affect the student's GPA and potentially influence future financial aid eligibility. Therefore, students should be well prepared and possess the discipline required to handle college-level work before enrolling.

The Experience of Dual Enrollment

For students who are academically inclined and prepared for college-level work, dual enrollment is an excellent option. My daughters, for instance, appreciated the flexibility of college courses and found that the writing and assignments aligned well with their interests. The experience also helped them develop time management skills that served them later, as college demands are significantly different from those of high school.

College dual enrollment offers homeschooled students a valuable introduction to higher education, providing them with a glimpse of what to expect and allowing them to determine if this path suits their academic and career goals.

Supporting Special Needs Learners

When it comes to educating special needs learners, the vast array of online resources available today can be incredibly beneficial, regardless of the student's level or specific needs. Embracing homeschooling for a special needs student can be a rewarding and effective option, provided you have the patience and commitment to make it work.

One benefit of homeschooling a special needs learner is the flexibility to take them to support appointments without interrupting valuable educational time. In public schools, students are often removed from their academic lessons for support services [like speech, occupational therapy, physical therapy, or academic supports]. I have seen this firsthand in my own daughter's schooling and working in a public school. As a homeschooling parent, you can create a schedule that allows for longer appointments, parent-directed/influenced outcomes, and no interruptions to valuable learning time.

Understanding the Benefits of Homeschooling a Special Needs Learner

Homeschooling offers significant advantages, including the ability to provide individualized attention and more time than a traditional school setting might allow. This personalized approach can make a substantial difference in your child's learning experience and outcomes. Additionally, homeschooling can offer a tailored environment that adapts to your child's unique needs and learning pace.

Exploring Available Resources

To make the most of homeschooling, it is crucial to tap into available resources and support systems.

1. **Local Programs and Funding**: While school districts may not always proactively share information about special needs resources, local homeschool organizations can be a valuable source of knowledge. Research the laws and programs in your state and county. Some states offer funds specifically for special needs learners that are accessible to both parents and school districts. These funds might be used for educational materials or support services.

2. **Scholarships and Vouchers**: In certain states, there are scholarships or vouchers available that can help cover the cost of private schools that accommodate special needs learners. These financial aids can also support hiring additional assistance, such as a behavioral aide, if needed. This is useful if you choose to do a hybrid homeschool.

3. **State Extended Standards**: Utilize state extended standards as a resource. For instance, in Ohio, extended standards provide a clearer breakdown of educational requirements and offer practical examples for teaching. These standards can serve as a foundational guide and can be adapted to create more complex learning activities as your student progresses.

4. **Online Platforms and Tools**: Platforms like Teachers Pay Teachers offer specialized resources for various levels of special needs, including vocational support lessons. These tools can be particularly useful for addressing more intensive needs. One drawback is that the TPT resources for students with special needs tend towards more cartoon and childish depictions. I found this very frustrating when looking for educational resources on life skill topics and social skills, in particular. You

may choose to purchase tools and modify to make them more age appropriate or take advantage of the leveled tools that we continue to develop on our website DecisionTreeLearning.com. If you don't see a tool you'd like to use, reach out to us. We may use your idea for a future resource.

Seeking Support and Collaboration

If you have specific needs or ideas for resources that could benefit your child, don't hesitate to reach out. We are constantly developing new materials and appreciate input from parents. By sharing your needs or ideas, you may receive tailored resources and contribute to the creation of new educational tools.

We welcome your feedback and suggestions. Contact us through our website's contact form. Your insights can help shape materials that assist not only your child but also others in similar situations.

Conclusion

Homeschooling special needs learners can be a fulfilling journey, enhanced by the wealth of online resources and support systems available. By exploring these resources, understanding local funding opportunities, and engaging with educational communities, you can provide a robust and supportive learning environment for your child. Remember, you're not alone in this endeavor—there are many resources and communities ready to assist and collaborate with you on this important journey.

Integrating Home Economics and Life Skills

Home economics and life skills are fundamental components of a child's education that can be introduced as early as elementary school. While more advanced aspects of these topics are covered in detail in the chapter on preparing your child for life beyond homeschooling, this chapter focuses on general life skills that can be implemented from a young age. I am trying to give you a few practical ideas to work these into your homeschool calendar.

Starting Early

Begin teaching home economics and life skills early. In our household, once our children could walk steadily, they were given simple chores. At around eighteen months to two years old, our kids started unloading the dishwasher. We placed plates in lower cabinets so they could reach them easily. As they grew older, their responsibilities expanded to putting away glasses and other items.

Incorporating chores into daily routines from a young age helps children develop essential life skills. Tasks such as bringing down laundry, folding it, and putting it away became a regular part of our children's lives. I didn't learn many of these skills until I was much older—like adulthood—and I found it very hard to create a workable routine because of this. I wanted it to be a natural part of life for my kids, just like getting ready in the morning, so they didn't have the same struggles I did. I believe that early exposure to home economics better prepares children for independence.

Practical Life Skills

Home economics encompasses a wide range of practical skills. Here are some ways to integrate these into your homeschooling:

1. **Grocery Lists and Meal Planning**: Involve your children in creating grocery lists and meal planning. Assign one child to plan meals for a day of the week each month. For example, our family had designated days for specific meals like fish, pasta, or soup. If you had a similar arrangement you could let a child choose recipes for those days and have them ensure we had the necessary ingredients. This teaches children how to manage grocery lists, budget, and plan meals effectively.

2. **Understanding Expenses**: Expose children to real-life financial scenarios. Teach them about the costs associated with groceries, utilities, and subscriptions. Discuss budgeting and saving and explain how unexpected expenses such as car repairs can impact a budget. This helps children understand the relationship between income and expenses and prepares them for financial responsibilities.

3. **Laundry and Household Chores**: Involve children in all aspects of laundry—starting, washing, folding, and putting away. These tasks are crucial for self-sufficiency and should be integrated into their daily routines.

4. **Bill Management**: As children approach their teenage years, introduce them to the concept of paying bills. Explain the costs of utilities, phone services, and subscriptions. This provides a realistic view of financial obligations and helps them understand the value of money. However, you don't need to wait that long to start with money management. My younger brother and I were introduced to budgeting in elementary school. We were given back-to-school budgets and could only spend the set amount to purchase all back-to-school supplies and clothes. This forced me to balance cost with quality and fads. It is a lesson I have

carried with me my entire life and passed to my children, one I learned when I was about 9 or 10 years old.

5. **Life Skills in Context**: Implement lessons that show cause and effect. For instance, if an unexpected expense arises, explain how it affects the budget and necessitates adjustments. This practical approach helps children grasp the importance of financial planning and adaptability. I realize some parents are concerned about this because they want to shield their children from worry. I'm sympathetic to that idea, but just because you don't show the full ramifications doesn't mean you cannot show that there is a small impact in their life—or that you had saved the money, thus averting the potential damage with preparation and saving, another positive life lesson.

Advanced Skills and Real-World Applications

As children mature, expand their learning to more complex concepts:

1. **Home Ownership and Maintenance**: Discuss the considerations of owning versus renting a home, including maintenance, decorating, and financial implications. Teach them about the costs of home ownership—such as down payments, mortgages, and property upkeep—along with the benefits, like tax deductions.

2. **Financial Literacy**: Include more formal lessons on financial literacy, such as understanding credit, debt, and real estate. Help them understand the implications of financial decisions and develop skills for managing personal finances. While many states are starting to require this, I strongly suggest going far beyond the minimum requirements of these education standards and include books on business, financial planning, and investment, in addition to home budgeting.

3. **Emergency Preparedness**: Teach children about emergency services, poison control, and basic first aid. These are essential life skills that can be integrated into daily routines and emergencies. Depending on weather in your area, discuss preparation for major weather events like hurricanes, tornadoes, blizzards, power outages, and even severe storms. People in earthquake or flood areas should include that. And remember to teach these skills for home as well as in a car. We teach kids about stranger danger when they are young; when they start to approach an age where they could be home alone, include these.

4. **Time Management**: Emphasize the importance of balancing responsibilities and leisure. Encourage children to use their time wisely, avoiding excessive entertainment that can lead to neglect of household tasks. Conversely, don't encourage a workaholic lifestyle that can lead to health challenges and destroy relationships. The key is to teach them to stay focused on what is in front of them rather than trying to multitask. Start the lessons by setting a good example for them and be honest when you struggle about the consequences.

By incorporating these skills into your homeschooling curriculum, you prepare children for a successful transition into adulthood. Start early and adapt the complexity of tasks as they grow. For additional resources and examples, visit our website. We are continually adding new material.

Integrating home economics and life skills into your homeschooling program not only prepares children for independence but also equips them with practical knowledge they will use throughout their lives.

Career Exploration for Homeschoolers

Career exploration is a crucial component of a well-rounded education, even at a young age. While this topic has been touched upon in other chapters, it's important to emphasize the role of career exploration in a student's development. This chapter will guide you through incorporating career exploration into your homeschooling routine, providing practical strategies and resources for helping students understand various professions and their requirements.

Introducing Career Exploration

Career exploration can begin as early as elementary school. One effective way to introduce this concept is through events like career day, where students learn about different professions. During these events, students can express their interests, and you can support their curiosity by exploring these fields further.

Researching Careers

Encourage your child to identify careers that intrigue them. If they are younger, you can find books about that job tailored to their age group. If they are older, have them gather information from various sources as part of a research or interview project. Visit the library for books on specific professions or use online resources such as YouTube to find videos about different jobs.

Part of this research is finding out what the job looks like in reality as opposed to the image. For example, do firefighters really go into burning buildings every single day or do they do other things? Does an engineer build a robot or sit at a desk? What does an autoworker's job look like on a daily basis? What jobs are available to a person with a commercial driver's license and what are the pros and cons of different kinds of driving jobs?

Delve into the specifics of each job. What skills and physical requirements are necessary? For instance, if a career involves laying pipes, consider the physical demands such as lifting heavy materials, working in confined spaces, or dealing with insects. Understanding these aspects will help students gain a realistic perspective on the job and, hopefully, have a better chance of finding a job that meets their needs and skills.

Utilizing Technology and Networking

Today's digital age offers unparalleled resources for career exploration. Encourage your child to use the internet to connect with professionals in their fields of interest [under your supervision]. A simple phone call or video chat with someone in the profession can provide valuable insights. You can do this by tapping into your network of friends and family who may be able to offer firsthand knowledge about various careers. Remember, as with all technology, be in the room and present for the interview.

Job Shadowing and Hands-On Experience

For older and more mature students, job shadowing can be an excellent opportunity to gain firsthand experience. Observing professionals in their work environment can help them determine if a particular career aligns with their interests and abilities.

Educational Pathways and Career Requirements

Once a student has identified a career of interest, it is essential to explore the educational and training requirements. Research what is needed to pursue that career path—whether it involves advanced degrees, on-the-job training, or specific certifications. For example, becoming a nurse practitioner requires a master's degree and is a very different job than being a nurse. Having a higher degree doesn't always mean a better, more enjoyable job. It is critical to understand the price that must be paid to get there as well as the tasks performed in a job to determine if it is a "good job." Furthermore, many jobs in the trades pay as much or more than jobs that require a college degree, so the idea of the past that college is the path to a great future isn't necessarily the case. That is why I emphasize so strongly learning about jobs and skills needed for those jobs rather than simply college preparedness.

Considering Lifestyle and Job Realities

Career exploration also involves examining the lifestyle associated with different professions. Consider factors such as work hours, job responsibilities, and salary. Some careers may require irregular hours or significant time commitments, which can impact a person's lifestyle and work-life balance.

Evaluate how these factors align with the student's personal goals and preferences. This exploration will help them understand the trade-offs involved and whether they are willing to make the necessary sacrifices.

Preparing for the Future

Encourage students who prefer to enter the job market directly after high school to consider how they can make themselves competitive. Research what skills and qualifications are needed for their desired job and how they can acquire them. If they will turn eighteen before completing their degree, consider setting up a co-op situation for them where they are working in that field prior to completing high school. There are many schools who do this by lengthening the school year or modifying the school day. Research how they can earn high school credit for work—probably as an elective—in your homeschool so that they still meet the requirements for your state to graduate. But, again, don't get trapped into thinking about a school year in a set way.

Flexibility and Adaptation

Keep in mind that career interests may change over time. Many people shift career paths, change majors, or even embark on second careers later in life. While it's important to provide guidance, it's equally important to allow flexibility and adaptability. As parents, in this part of our child's life, we need to be facilitators, not in control.

Integrating Career Exploration into Homeschooling

Incorporate career exploration into your homeschooling curriculum in a way that fits your family's routine. This doesn't have to be a formal class; it could be part of a life skills course, a series of lessons, or special projects. By making career exploration an ongoing part of your homeschooling experience, you help students gain valuable insights and make informed decisions about their futures.

Special Interest Projects in Homeschooling

Special interest projects are one of the most compelling aspects of homeschooling, offering unique opportunities for deeper learning and personal growth. These projects, which span extended periods, are a powerful tool for teaching time management skills—an essential ability that is often overlooked in traditional educational settings.

In conventional schools, students are typically guided through daily schedules where teachers dictate the day's activities and homework assignments. The concept of long-term projects, where students manage their time and progress over a week or more, isn't often emphasized. Special interest projects fill this gap by requiring students to engage in activities that extend beyond a single day or week. For younger children, these projects might last a week, but as students grow older, they can undertake projects that span a month, a semester, or even the entire school year.

Reflecting on my own educational experience from the 1980s, I attended a school that embraced individually guided education. This approach involved students managing their own learning paths with guidance from teachers. For instance, in math classes, we began with a collective review of chapter one, but thereafter, we were responsible for progressing through the remaining chapters at our own pace. Our progress was assessed through pretests and posttests, allowing us to focus on areas where we needed improvement without having to redo entire chapters.

This approach instilled in me strong time management skills that proved invaluable in high school and college. Special interest projects operate on a similar principle, allowing students to explore their interests deeply and practice skills to learn to manage their time effectively.

These projects can vary in length and complexity. They might be brief, lasting a week or a month, or more extensive, spanning an entire semester or school year. It is beneficial to introduce multiple projects at the beginning of the fall term. Start with smaller projects to build skills and gradually increase the scope as students gain experience. These projects can be integrated into various subjects, such as a research paper for social studies or a science fair project that aligns with classwork.

Younger students might need more guidance initially. You can assist them in selecting a topic, brainstorming ideas, and outlining their project. As they gain experience, they should be encouraged to plan their projects more independently. This includes defining their research goals, methodology, and presentation format. I continue to create homeschool resources to help teach these skills if you don't feel confident in how to do them. Make sure you receive the Decision Tree Learning newsletter, so you find out when new resources are available. [Visit our website DecisionTreeLearning.com to sign up.]

Maintaining a special interest project journal is an effective way for students to track their progress. This journal can be a simple notebook or composition book where they record their ideas, deadlines, and reflections on their work. The process of documenting and reviewing their progress helps them develop organizational skills and resilience. It is important for students to understand that failure is not a setback but an opportunity to learn and adapt. This perspective is crucial for fostering a growth mindset.

Encourage students to see failure as a natural part of the learning process. Just as athletes refine their techniques or artists adjust their methods, students should view mistakes as chances to improve their approach and enhance their problem-solving skills.

To further enrich special interest projects, consider setting a budget for materials. For instance, you might allocate a certain amount of money for a semester-long project, requiring students to plan their purchases and manage their resources. This introduces practical life skills such as budgeting, sourcing materials, and organizing their workspace.

Incorporating special interest projects into your homeschooling routine can bring together various disciplines—math, science, reading, career exploration, study skills, and critical thinking—into a cohesive learning experience. Whether students are exploring a personal interest or discovering new areas of curiosity, these projects offer a valuable opportunity for comprehensive, hands-on learning.

To support your efforts, our website provides resources, including project templates, rubrics, and guides for evaluating and grading these projects. Embrace the flexibility and creativity that special interest projects bring to homeschooling and make them a regular and enjoyable part of your educational approach.

Chapter 21: Mastering Study Skills

Effective study skills are crucial for academic success, with note-taking being a fundamental component. This chapter outlines effective note-taking techniques and review strategies tailored to different educational levels.

Note-Taking and Study Skills

Study skills are essential tools for academic success, and effective note-taking is a cornerstone of these skills. This chapter will guide you through the best practices for note-taking and review strategies, tailored to different educational levels. While this section is for the homeschooling parent to read, I've really written this to the students, so they can learn how to master the art of note-taking, reviewing, and studying.

Note-Taking Strategies

Early Elementary

In the early elementary years, note-taking involves recording essential information to aid understanding and memory. Start by writing down key vocabulary words and their definitions, as well as assignment deadlines. This practice helps students stay organized and keep track of their responsibilities.

When in class, make sure to jot down names of important people and new terms introduced by the teacher. For example, if you learn about George Washington, you might write: "George Washington - leader of the colonial forces in the Revolutionary War, first U.S. president." Similarly, record key dates and events, such as "July 4, 1776 - Declaration of Independence" and "Boston Tea Party - a protest against British taxation."

Mnemonics are also helpful at this stage. For instance, the mnemonic "My Very Educated Mother Just Served Us Nine Pickles" helps recall the planets in our solar system. Even though Pluto is no longer classified as a planet, such mnemonics assist in memorizing and organizing information.

Upper Grades

As students progress to upper grades, note-taking becomes more detailed. In addition to names and dates, focus on capturing processes and additional information provided by the teacher. Record everything from the board, handouts, and lectures. This comprehensive approach ensures that all relevant details are included.

Reviewing Your Notes

Effective note-taking is just the beginning; reviewing your notes is crucial for reinforcement and retention. Review your notes daily or shortly after class to address any incomplete thoughts or unclear sections. Fill in gaps and ensure that your notes accurately reflect the day's lessons.

To highlight key information, use colored pencils or crayons instead of highlighters, which can bleed through the paper. Look for and mark important dates, names, and cause-and-effect relationships. For step-by-step processes, use color-coding or symbols to connect related steps, making it easier to locate and understand them later.

Creating Review Materials

After reviewing your notes, the next step is to create review materials. This could involve rewriting important information clearly in a review journal, creating flashcards, or developing review sheets. In your review journal, summarize processes and key concepts, organizing them into bullet points for clarity.

Schedule regular review sessions—weekly or more frequently if needed—depending on the amount of material and the structure of your homeschooling. During these sessions, focus on synthesizing information and reinforcing your understanding of the material.

Preview, Learn, and Review

Adopt a structured approach to learning: preview, learn, and review. Preview the material before class by skimming through the textbook or notes. This helps you to become familiar with key concepts and terms so that when they are introduced in class, you are prepared and can follow along more effectively.

During the learning phase, take detailed notes, ask questions, and engage actively with the material. After class, review your notes and create review materials to consolidate your understanding and retention.

By following these strategies, students can enhance their study skills, improve their note-taking, and effectively review and retain information.

Chapter 22: Additional Resources

My website DecisionTreeLearning.com is the best source for updates and additional resources to help you homeschool. We have updates, discounted and exclusive products, signups for our affiliate program, and much more. In this section, we have included some of the resources mentioned throughout the book to help you organize your homeschool. We are always creating new lessons and would love to hear from you about resources and subjects that would help you in your homeschooling. Use our contact page on our website or respond to our newsletter with your suggestions.

Field Trip Sheets

Field trips are a great way to learn outside the classroom, and having a field trip sheet is a great way to focus your child to make it a learning experience. The sheets should include descriptions, a specific thing to look out for, something that has been of interest to the child, a recently covered topic, or something similar based on your purpose in going on the field trip. What I love about this is it shows that learning things is what we do every day—not just in a formalized environment. As the homeschool parent, you can then point out that discovering something you didn't know or taking special note of something is learning. The sheet focuses that new information in our brain and can serve as a fun memento.

Field Trip sheet

Location:_____

Date:_____

Assignment:

Something I enjoyed:

Tools to Help Homeschooling Parents

Homeschool Schedule Creation

In order to make sure all subjects are covered during the course of the week, I've created a tool called the "Student Schedule Planning Sheet." These are included in our homeschool planner, *Your Homeschool Blueprint*, but I've included one here for you to have as a sample. For each student, you can keep track of all of the elements of your homeschool. The weekends are included since some people have church choir practice for part of their music requirements or weekend dance lessons for PE. This will help you have an organized way to plan your weekly schooling lessons for each child and not be overwhelmed by trying to do too many subjects in a single day. This can be used in conjunction with the Student Schedule Planning Sheet.

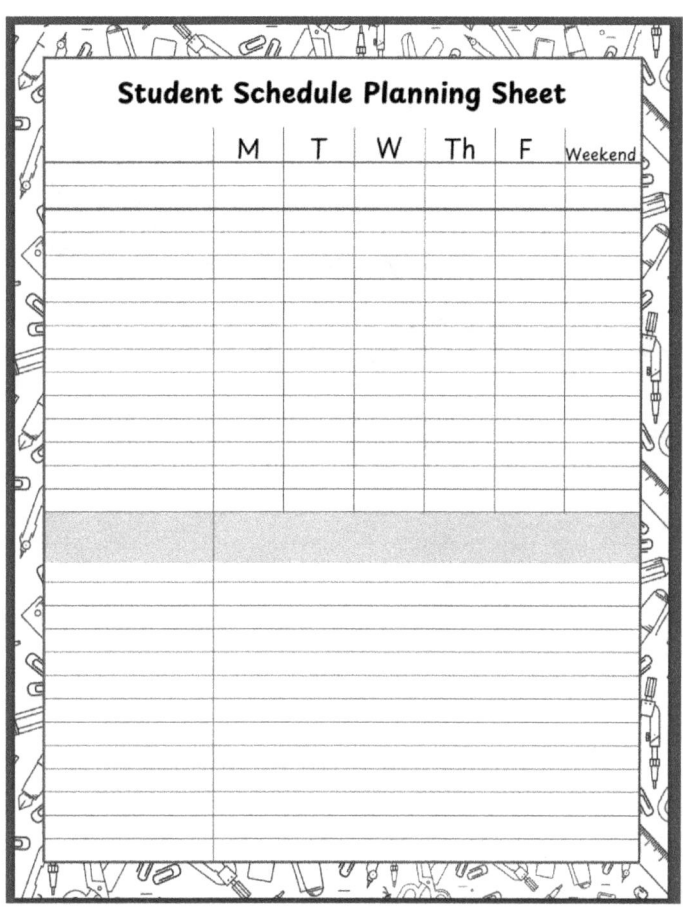

The Preview, Learn, Review Tool:

STUDENT _____
WEEK #
DATE :

✦ *for this week* ✦
Learning Cycle

Subject/topic	PREVIEW	LEARN	REVIEW	ASSESS

To use this tool to track material for each student during the week, I suggest writing the subject or topic on the left. Then you can put a day of the week, and assignment, lesson, task or another indicator below each column. This will prevent you from grouping assessments on a single day, but rather ensuring that there is a good mix of various learning stages each day and in each course. You have 4 rather than 5 boxes in a week which allows additional time for any of the steps each learing cycle. Make sure Monday is not always a preview day for all subjects, but rather each subject has its own 4-7 school day cycle based on student needs.

Rubric Creation Tool and Sample Rubrics

To create your own rubric, you need to consider a few factors:

- What skills do you want your child to learn?
- What will demonstrate proof of learning or levels of progress?
- What factors are critical for completing the task well?

With this in mind, you will then divide the levels of demonstration of mastery [between three and five], divide the key skills and factors, and create a matrix of these.

Sample Rubric for a Science Fair Project

Demonstration of mastery:

In this example we'll have four point levels: 0, 1–3, 4–7, 8–10

Skills I want the child to learn:

- Presentation [oral explanation and answering questions]
- Presentation [physical project, clarity, appearance, data presentation]
- Scientific inquiry [What were they investigating and did they approach it seriously and scientifically?]

So, for each of these categories I will determine what is sufficient and clearly define it. For example:

Student had a physical presentation that showed the data collected in a reasonable format that only left a few questions about what was studied. Some images supporting the research were present and the font was readable.

This would be in the 4–7 range, so a point number between four and seven would be given based on this criteria. Notice how I very clearly explained to the student some of the key components I wanted present on their physical project [this requirement should also be outlined in the assignment], but it is reiterated on the rubric.

You would then define what kind of criteria would warrant an 8–10. A zero would be reserved for "this component was not present."

I have given sample rubrics for all grades, K–12, to get you started. The easiest way to create a rubric, in my opinion, is to create it as you're writing [or reading through] an assignment.

The requirements articulated in the assignment should be the guidelines of the rubric. Assign points based on what you feel demonstrates basic, average, and advanced levels of comprehension. Keep in mind that an *average* is a C, not an A. A is for well above average mastery of material. While I never advocate being cruel or unreasonable in grading, I likewise don't advocate for inflated, unreasonable grading. Both are damaging.

Lower Elementary (1st–3rd Grade) Grading Rubric

Skill	5-6 points	3-4 points	1-2 points	0 points
Identifying the problem	Clearly identifies the problem in a simple and understanding way, showing basic understanding of the issue	Identifies the problem but lacks clarity or depth; may need some help to fully understand it.	Struggles to identify the problem, or only mentions it in passing without showing understanding	Did not identify the problem
Determining Whether the Problem Should be Addressed	Shows clear thinking about whether the problem should be solved and considers how it might affect different people.	Understands that the problem needs a solution but doesn't fully consider how it affects everyone.	Struggles to decide whether the problem should be addressed or doesn't consider the effects on others.	Did not determine whether or not the problem should be addressed
Sharing Who is Affected by the Problem	Names who is affected by the problem, showing awareness of the impact on others.	Mentions some people affected but doesn't fully explain how they are impacted.	Only briefly mentions others, or doesn't clearly explain who is affected.	Did not share who is affected by the problem
Identifying Solutions	Suggests a clear and simple solution to the problem, showing creative thinking.	Suggests a solution, but it may be incomplete or not fully thought out.	Struggles to come up with a solution, or the solution is unclear or unrealistic.	Did not identify solutions
Identifying Who is Impacted if There is a Solution	Explains how the solution will help others, showing understanding of the positive effects.	Mentions some positive impacts but doesn't fully explain them.	Does not clearly explain the positive impact of the solution.	Did not identify who is impacted if there is a solution
Identifying Who is Impacted if There is No Solution	Understands and explains what might happen if the problem isn't solved, showing concern for those affected.	Mentions some consequences but doesn't fully explain them.	Doesn't clearly explain what will happen if the problem isn't solved.	Did not identify who is impacted if there is no solution

Upper Elementary (4th-6th Grade) Grading Rubric

Skill	8-10 points	4-7 points	1-3 points
Identifying the problem	Clearly identifies the problem, showing an understanding of the issue and its importance.	Identifies the problem but may lack depth or clarity in explanation.	Struggles to identify the problem or only mentions it in a superficial way.
Sharing Who is Affected by the Problem	Accurately describes who is affected by the problem and how it impacts them.	Identifies some affected groups but doesn't fully explain the impact.	Mentions who is affected in a vague or incomplete manner.
Determining Whether the Problem Should be Addressed	Thoughtfully considers whether the problem should be solved, weighing the benefits and potential drawbacks.	Understands the need to solve the problem but doesn't fully consider all perspectives.	Struggles to make a clear decision or doesn't consider the broader impact of solving the problem.
Identifying Solutions	Proposes a logical and thoughtful solution to the problem, showing creativity or insight.	Suggests a solution but may not fully explain how it addresses the problem.	Suggests an unclear or incomplete solution.
Identifying Who is Impacted if There is a Solution	Thoroughly explains how the solution will benefit others and addresses the positive outcomes.	Mentions some positive outcomes but lacks depth in explanation.	Does not clearly explain the benefits of the solution or provides an incomplete explanation.
Identifying Who is Impacted if There is No Solution	Clearly explains the potential consequences of not solving the problem, showing understanding of the stakes.	Mentions some consequences but does not fully explore them.	Only briefly mentions consequences or shows little understanding of the impacts.

Middle School Rubric

Skill	10-12 points	7-9 points	1-6 points
Identifying the problem	Clearly identifies the problem, showing an understanding of the issue and its importance.	Identifies the problem but may lack depth or clarity in explanation.	Struggles to identify the problem or only mentions it in a superficial way.
Sharing Who is Affected by the Problem	Accurately describes who is affected by the problem and how it impacts them.	Identifies some affected groups but doesn't fully explain the impact.	Mentions who is affected in a vague or incomplete manner.
Determining Whether the Problem Should be Addressed	Thoughtfully considers whether the problem should be solved, weighing the benefits and potential drawbacks.	Understands the need to solve the problem but doesn't fully consider all perspectives.	Struggles to make a clear decision or doesn't consider the broader impact of solving the problem.
Identifying Solutions	Proposes a logical and thoughtful solution to the problem, showing creativity or insight.	Suggests a solution but may not fully explain how it addresses the problem.	Suggests an unclear or incomplete solution.
Identifying Who is Impacted if There is a Solution	Thoroughly explains how the solution will benefit others and addresses the positive outcomes.	Mentions some positive outcomes but lacks depth in explanation.	Does not clearly explain the benefits of the solution or provides an incomplete explanation.
Identifying Who is Impacted if There is No Solution	Clearly explains the potential consequences of not solving the problem, showing understanding of the stakes.	Mentions some consequences but does not fully explore them.	Only briefly mentions consequences or shows little understanding of the impacts.

High School Rubric

Skill	13-15 points	9-12 points	1-8 points
Identifying the problem	Clearly identifies the problem with deep analysis and understanding, showing awareness of its complexity.	Identifies the problem with reasonable clarity, though the analysis may lack some depth.	Struggles to clearly identify the problem, providing only a basic or surface-level understanding.
Sharing Who is Affected by the Problem	Accurately identifies and thoroughly explains who is affected by the problem and how they are impacted.	Identifies affected groups but may not fully explore the extent of the impact.	Provides a superficial or incomplete explanation of who is affected.
Determining Whether the Problem Should be Addressed	Thoughtfully evaluates the need to solve the problem, carefully weighing the benefits and potential drawbacks for different groups.	Considers the need to solve the problem but may not fully explore the implications for all groups.	Struggles to make a clear decision or does not consider the broader implications of solving the problem.
Identifying Solutions	Proposes well-reasoned and creative solutions that address the problem from multiple angles.	Suggests solutions that address the problem but may lack thoroughness or creativity.	Provides basic or incomplete solutions that may not fully address the problem.
Identifying Who is Impacted if There is a Solution	Provides a detailed and thoughtful explanation of the positive outcomes of the solution, considering various groups.	Identifies positive outcomes but may not fully explore the broader impacts.	Provides a basic or incomplete explanation of the positive outcomes.
Identifying Who is Impacted if There is No Solution	Clearly explains the potential consequences of not solving the problem, showing understanding of the broader impact.	Mentions some consequences but does not fully explore the broader impacts.	Provides only a superficial explanation of the potential negative consequences.

College Level Rubric

Skill	16-20 points	11-15 points	1-10 points
Identifying the problem	Clearly and comprehensively identifies the problem, demonstrating deep understanding and sophisticated analysis.	Identifies the problem with clarity but may not fully explore all nuances or complexities.	Struggles to clearly identify the problem, providing only a surface-level understanding or missing key aspects.
Sharing Who is Affected by the Problem	Thoroughly identifies and analyzes who is affected by the problem, demonstrating an understanding of the issue's broader impact on multiple groups.	Identifies affected groups but may not fully explore or analyze the depth of the impact.	Provides a basic or incomplete explanation of who is affected, lacking depth in analysis.
Determining Whether the Problem Should be Addressed	Thoughtfully evaluates the necessity of solving the problem, carefully weighing the benefits, costs, and ethical considerations for all groups involved.	Considers the need to solve the problem but may not fully explore the implications for all groups or the potential trade-offs.	Struggles to make a clear decision or does not consider the broader implications, costs, or ethical considerations of solving the problem.
Identifying Solutions	Proposes well-reasoned, innovative solutions that address the problem comprehensively, considering multiple perspectives and potential obstacles.	Suggests solutions that address the problem but may lack depth, creativity, or consideration of all relevant factors.	Provides basic or incomplete solutions that do not fully address the problem or lack critical thinking.
Identifying Who is Impacted if There is a Solution	Provides a detailed and nuanced explanation of the positive outcomes of the solution, considering both immediate and long-term impacts on various groups.	Identifies positive outcomes but may not fully explore or analyze the broader impacts.	Provides a basic or incomplete explanation of the positive outcomes, lacking depth or insight.
Identifying Who is Impacted if There is No Solution	Clearly and thoroughly explains the broader consequences of not solving the problem, considering long-term and short-term impacts on various groups.	Mentions some consequences but may not fully explore or analyze the broader impacts.	Provides a superficial explanation of the potential negative consequences, lacking depth or insight.

About the Author

Tiffany Colter has been a professional writer and business coach for over two decades. She has successfully homeschooled her children, tutored students in standardized college entrance tests, worked with students at various levels on the autism spectrum, and worked with teachers in moderate to intense and unit classrooms. She has more than seven years of experience supporting teachers in helping students with special needs who also have communication challenges and delays. Tiffany has developed innovative tools, such as those on the Decision Tree Learning website, to assist both parents and teachers with resources for students in a variety of topics—and growing. These resources are suitable for students in general education, students in supported classrooms [from mild to intense], teachers in home instruction settings, and parents in homeschool settings.

Tiffany's life was heavily impacted by a series of highly influential teachers and mentors, and because of this she has a drive to help parents, teachers, and students. "I believe in the power of applied knowledge," Tiffany will often say. So many teachers and parents want to help kids learn, but with the requirements from administrators and financial limitations, it can feel overwhelming to try to create tools that will engage students' interest. Parents can be overwhelmed homeschooling their children at different grade levels simultaneously. This is where Tiffany saw a need she could fill. While a homeschooling mom, she felt limited in what she could do by time, finances, and mental fatigue—and many times all three simultaneously. Now she creates a growing library of engaging content leveled from advanced general education to students working at the simplest level of extended standards. These affordable materials are offered on her website.

Tiffany's path was not linear. Like many parents, she often felt overwhelmed by the demands of homeschooling, managing a household, and running a business. She understands firsthand the complexities of balancing professional goals, family life, and personal health. These challenges, along with her resilience, have shaped her empathetic and practical approach to coaching and content creation. She offers real-world strategies for parents, teachers, and homeschoolers to navigate the demands of daily life while providing creative projects, leveled learning, and social skills to a very diverse population.

In addition to her work with individual families, Tiffany has a deep understanding of the needs within special education classrooms. She has collaborated with teachers as a sign language facilitator to enhance communication and learning for students with diverse abilities. Her Decision Tree Learning framework helps parents and educators break down complex concepts into manageable steps, empowering children to learn in various environments, from public and private schools to homeschool settings.

Tiffany's dedication to helping others extends beyond education. Through her various platforms, she continues to create resources that support parents in explaining difficult concepts to their children, while providing teachers with tools to meet individual needs in the classroom. Her ever-expanding catalog of learning materials is adaptable, budget-friendly, and designed to meet the unique needs of children in any learning environment.

With a passion for education, writing, and entrepreneurship, Tiffany Colter embodies the drive to help others achieve success while maintaining balance in all aspects of life. Through her guidance, countless individuals have found ways to foster growth in their children.

About DecisionTreeLearning.com

Decision Tree Learning provides innovative lessons and curriculum solutions that encourage critical thinking abilities and embrace the learning process. These comprehensive and affordable resources are made available to educators, parents, and homeschooling families at a steep discount on DecisionTreeLearning.com or at full retail at a variety of online retailers.

At Decision Tree Learning, we believe that embracing failure is a necessary step on the path to success. Our courses are made to help students become resilient and persistent, to view obstacles as chances for personal development rather than as something to be feared, and to recognize the power of applied knowledge in every area of their lives.

Since each learner is different, our website accommodates a wide range of demands, including those of special learners—like those with autism, apraxia, or ADHD—as well as older students. Our unique curricula contain courses that are tiered to accommodate both persons with moderate to severe communication and comprehension issues and students learning in conventional and accelerated classes.

Our website is developing into a library of thorough curricula, videos, podcasts, and lessons covering academic skills, communication skills, vocational skills, and life skills as we continue to add new resources over the course of the next year. This will ensure that learners have the tools they need to succeed in every aspect of their lives. In addition, we will provide parents and educators with strategies to assist you in reaching your student, regardless of how engaged they are. We are in the trenches with the teacher, homeschooling parent, and lifelong learner, supporting you as you help your students.

Decision Tree Learning offers a comprehensive approach to education, encompassing social communication skills development, reading comprehension, arithmetic concept mastery, life/social skills support, and vocational skills development.

www.ingramcontent.com/pod-product-compliance
Lightning Source LLC
Chambersburg PA
CBHW060837190426
43197CB00040B/2659